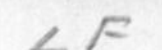

Voices in the Whirlwind and Other Essays

Voices in the Whirlwind

AND OTHER ESSAYS

BY EZEKIEL MPHAHLELE

HILL AND WANG NEW YORK
A division of Farrar, Straus and Giroux

ISBN (CLOTHBOUND EDITION): 0-8090-9627-7
ISBN (PAPERBACK EDITION): 0-8090-1361-4
LIBRARY OF CONGRESS CATALOG CARD NUMBER: 70-163568
PUBLISHED SIMULTANEOUSLY BY DOUBLEDAY CANADA LTD., TORONTO
MANUFACTURED IN THE UNITED STATES OF AMERICA
2 3 4 5 6 7 8 9 10

"African Literature: What Tradition?" originally appeared in the *Denver Quarterly*

"The Fabric of African Cultures" originally appeared in *Foreign Affairs*. Copyright © 1964 by the Council on Foreign Relations, Inc.

"African Writers and Commitment" originally appeared as "Writers and Commitment" in *Black Orpheus*

"Censorship in South Africa" originally appeared in *Censorship Today*

FOR DENNIS BRUTUS:

You stopped a fascist bullet.

FOR KGOSITSILE:

Your "borrowed fears"
are also mine—
and so your questionings.

FOR GWENDOLYN BROOKS:

Thanks for the incisive image.
You are a focus of
the many streams of Black reality;
Your heart straddles
the times of unobtrusive grief
to times of rage;
rendering the drama
You bring home the meaning.

FOR CHABI AND PUSO:

My youngest two:
the whirlwind's coming
to meet you
my sons.
Don't ever let it hug you
twist you hurt you.
It's none too soon
to learn the signs:
see that bird over there
poised on a wingspan
to ride the storm—
the bird knows its enemies:
that's the abc of it,
sons.
It's never too soon.

Contents

Voices in the Whirlwind: Poetry and Conflict in the Black World

In 1945 I began teaching English and Afrikaans in a Johannesburg high school. The students did not use textbooks. The teacher wrote poems out of his textbook on the board for students to copy into a hardcover notebook. They had then to look for pictures in magazines and so on to paste in their books, taking care that the picture that the student thought "illustrated" a poem appeared on the page opposite the text. You might thus find a picture of an ox-drawn covered wagon (a symbol of the frontier days of Boer life) opposite a vitriolic anti-British, anti-African poem in Afrikaans! The school inspectors who, in that supervisory position, had to be white gave marks for the way the student had arranged his anthology and the pictures he used. Then there was an oral examination, during which the students were to recite some of the verses from memory. We found out that white children were taught in the same way in their schools.

At the matriculation level—the last two years of high school—we used printed texts for poetry courses. Students were expected to be taught to appreciate poetry—after three years of desperately trying to see poetry in pictorial terms! Again, at this stage, Africans wrote the same examinations as the whites, although in separate schools. It was a ridiculous and frustrating method of teaching poetry. The whites did not question it. When we, the Africans, could have, we were plunged into educational politics involving the rejection of a system of inferior schooling the government was imposing on blacks—an inferior curriculum now sanctioned by law. But that is another story.

Twelve years later, when I taught English literature in the Department of Extramural studies at the University of Ibadan, Nigeria, I came face to face with the problem of teaching poetry to adults, most of whom wanted to finish high school and thereby improve their marketability in employment. I realized that they had been taught merely to recite poetry in the earlier years of their schooling. What kind of poetry? Wordsworth (including "Daffodils"), Tennyson, Keats, and so on!

An idea struck me that I might begin by leading them through an inquiry into poetry as a heightened and condensed form of expression, whether in verse or prose. I had to lead them to the idea of poetry as *a state of mind* first. They had to understand that poetry was nothing new to Africa (which surprised them!), that every human being of average intelligence has poetic states of mind at different times, i.e., every person, literate or illiterate, at one time or another perceives things and events poetically. He sees something behind the initial stimulus, or meanings radiate or vibrate from the thing perceived; that what we *read* as poetry is merely the work of the literate, a sophisticated activity.

What better way of demonstrating these states of mind than by examining African idiomatic speech? So I asked each student to write down as many metaphors and proverbs as he could think up, each in the original language. Then they were to give a literal English translation for the benefit of the whole class. We examined several of these items of figurative speech. It became clear to the class that each time a person uttered such speech in everyday life, it was either in circumstances of ritual or it was a way of lending gravity or importance to what was being said, even in humorous circumstances. The speaker would be wanting to strike at more meanings than one at any time. There was a conscious or unconscious attempt to synthesize, to see things as a whole, made up of interconnected elements.

A saying from my own language (Sesotho) that is used by a man's representatives during negotiations for a bride is "We have come to ask for a calabash." This is part of a ritual. It accentuates, like the rest of the poetry that will be used from then on, the gravity of the moment, the sense of traditional propriety. A calabash holds fresh water or milk or beer—all sources of nourishment, a possible expression of generosity. These suggest the woman's womb, her giving and receiving capacities. The calabash is smooth on the outside: a woman should have such a smooth skin that a tear should roll down easily on it. The calabash is fragile: a woman should not be kicked around.

When a guest has eaten enough and his host wants to know, the former will say, "Yes, after all you do not eat until you grow horns."

At this point, the students relive poetry at its basic level. We go on to African oral poetry and then on to the written poetry of Africa and other parts of the world. By now we have come to grasp the idea of poetry as a language.

This method has never failed me: it worked for me and younger participants at subsequent writers' workshops in East Africa.

My encounter with American Negro poetry set me thinking about a number of things: it set me asking further questions about the meaning and function of poetry. So I embarked upon the exploration that follows. It is a poetry born out of situations of political controversy or conflict. And I want to find out how the American Negro poetic performance seeks to answer the questions implied in the goals so much of it has set for itself. The African poetry is included for purposes of comparison. It it a verse that consciously challenges political authority, which in turn differs from territory to territory, from culture to culture. David Diop pits himself against French colonial authority; Dennis Brutus stands opposed to white authority that is based not overseas but in South Africa itself; Wole Soyinka's conflict is with a newly established black authority.

I am also aware that my earlier students of poetry will be wrestling with the same problems, once having gone over the hurdle of understanding the workings of poetry as a language, the basic roots of it: problems concerning poetry that, consciously or unconsciously, seeks to meet sociopolitical imperatives of a contemporary order; problems concerning overtly public poetry and that which arrives at a communal sensibility via the individual experience or vision of the writer.

The world has been searching for the meaning of poetry for centuries. But in each phase of history we find ourselves asking what poetry does or can do for mankind. Because at each stage we find our physical and other needs and wants have grown more complex and problematic. We feel disoriented and confused. We look back in tradition to see whether some of its lessons apply to our time. We have long given up the idea that was noisily started by the F. R. Leavis set and published in *Scrutiny* in 1932—the idea that "there is a necessary relationship between the quality of the individual's response to art and his general fitness for a humane existence." Neither our perception of the "unified sensibility" in literature nor the critic's revelation of this seems to have influenced for the better the corporate will of a society, even in countries where literature has been produced in written form for centuries. It has not, for instance, been a brake on the march of racism, fascism, the acquisitive drive and its corollary, the rat race, in developed countries.

When African and other pre-industrial communities in the world recited praise poetry and folk tales, sang ballads, dramatized healing processes, ancestral worship; when society had not yet disintegrated, there could never have been talk about a "unified sensibility": it was a natural thing. Now the world is divided into camps—capitalists, socialists, the haves and have-nots, Protestants, Catholics, humanists, workers, employers, agnostics, atheists, Mohammedans, Hindus, Buddhists, blacks, whites, pacifists, and so on—conflict has become the order of the day, even while economics blur some of the frontiers. Poetry is a state of mind, so it tends to be a ready tool for the expression or dramatization of protest and indignation and exhortation for many who regard themselves as poets. And we write a poetry we hope will communicate emotion, move our readers in some direction, or sharpen their awareness.

From the point of view of the poet's art, what has he lost since the days of the Homeric epic, of the ballad or of the praise poem? Certainly the Western world possesses what Eric Heller calls a "disinherited mind." It has lost the mythology of ancient times that reaffirmed and strengthened man's beliefs. The poet is now creating new symbols, often ones that exist only in the private sector of his mind. Some of the symbols are obscure and so a poet's verse becomes partially or wholly incomprehensible. Indeed, since the 1930's Western poetry, especially that of the white world, has become a mere intellectual juggling, or, as another critic calls it, "intellectual frivolity," "clever meaninglessness." [1] But we in Africa are, like the Orient, still close to our mythology and oral poetry. We are drawing images from them for our contemporary poetry. The slow deliberate speech of an elder spokesman and a pastoral-elegiac mood are clearly captured in Kofi Awoonor's "Songs of Sorrow." [2]

Dzogbese Lisa* has treated me thus
It has led me among the shafts of the forest
Returning is not possible
And going forward is a great difficulty
The affairs of this world are like the chameleon faeces
Into which I have stepped
When I clean it cannot go
I am on the world's extreme corner
I am not sitting in the row with the eminent
But those who are lucky
Sit in the middle and forget
I am on the world's extreme corner
I can only go beyond and forget . . .

John Pepper Clark exploits the image of Olokun, the Yoruba goddess of the sea, generous to all men. He and Wole Soyinka

1. D. J. Enright, *The Apothecary's Shop* (London: Secker and Warburg, 1957).
2. From Gerald Moore and Ulli Beier (eds.), *Modern Poetry from Africa* (Harmondsworth: Penguin, 1963), p. 78.
* Fate.

use the *abiku* image to stand for different qualities. An *abiku* is a child born to die young and to return again and again to be born to the same mother. Clark pleads to him to stay and not go; Soyinka's *abiku* boasts that he cannot be held on earth ("the god's swollen foot")[3] not for all the bangles, cowries, and so on that they can offer him. There are several other examples of this dialogue between the present and living traditions in Africa. Shall we also one day experience "the disinherited mind"?

And yet basically the poet today is doing the same thing his predecessor did in the old days before his art began to be subjected to a variety of technical manipulations, some freakish, others a sincere act of revolt, seeking to release poetic form to correspond to a release of energy in the poet himself. For all the modes poetry has moved through over the ages, it still leaves us with the impression that we are hearing in a lyric something like a communal voice, coming across to us through an individual experience. "Poetry," says Christopher Caudwell, "is a bundle of instinctive perspectives of reality taken from one spot. . . . In it the instincts give one loud cry, a cry which expresses what is common in the general relation of every man to contemporary life as a whole." [4]

From "one spot" means both the poet as an individual and the point from which he begins to perceive. The poet wants to express himself, in other words, to extend himself in relation to society. In so doing he articulates his private experience in such a form that it can become part of the world of art as a work of art itself. He has thus forced his new experience into the field of consciousness, out of the area where it was dumb, unformulated. His consciousness is bound to change because of the entry of the experience through the medium of art into the world. The contemplator of art himself is bound to be affected; if the art is good, his consciousness will be shaken by the entry

3. *Ibid.*, p. 118.

4. Christopher Caudwell, *Illusion and Reality: A Study of the Sources of Poetry* (Delhi: People's Publishing House, 1956), p. 206. Reprinted by permission of the publisher.

of a new work of art into it. If he can identify with it because it represents an experience he is familiar with, however vaguely, he will appreciate the art work.

Poetry, Caudwell explains, springs from the contradiction between the instincts and experience of the poet. The same language the poet uses to express his private emotions also expresses the nature of the objective existence of experience:

> Hence poetry in some form is as eternal to society as man's struggle with Nature, a struggle of which association in economic production is the outcome. In poetry itself this takes the form of man entering into emotional communion with his fellow men by retiring into himself.[5]

The experiences of a community or society converge in the poet and condition his consciousness. He experiences something as an individual and a contradiction sets in between this private experience and the sum of experiences of his fellow men. This tension between his private instincts and his social environment has to be resolved. It happens when he expresses himself and makes his personal voice represent the public voice, when he can express his private experience in terms of that of the community, or vice versa. And so the public voice is heard even while we know the poet is struggling to articulate his private experience and the emotion or emotions it evokes in him. Poetry, or any other art, is thus integrated, unifying personal and communal instinctive drives. The "I" is "we," the "me" is "us" in poetry.

The item of private experience has to be *important,* concerned with emotions in depth, with those instincts in us that are man's permanent equipment from the cradle to the grave; yet it has to be *general,* peculiar to society in general, not just to the poet or one or two men; to be found "dumb unconscious in the experiences of most men." Great art thus endures because it integrates private instincts with those common to man in general within a cultural context. This integration explains why art has such meaning for us. Caudwell seems to take for granted

5. *Ibid.,* p. 126.

as an additional element that makes great art enduring the *memorable* idiom in which it is cast. As Auden says, poetry is "memorable speech." I can't assess a poem merely or purely on the basis of the technical skill or craftsmanship it displays, or merely as a kind of music box. It has to say something meaningful to me. Caudwell, however, implies "memorable speech" in what he says about the significance of word associations or imagery and the ambiguity that emerges from these. Speech in poetry is memorable, he suggests, because the mind forms associations of the words *immediately,* instead of first referring to the object symbolized by the word and then letting the associations radiate from that. As words are fewer than the objects they symbolize, the language of poetry has to be condensed. In responding to and interpreting this language, the instinctive part of a reader's consciousness is set alive, and thus he can grasp the various layers of meaning in a poem not readily within reach of the fully conscious part of the mind.

Caudwell clinches his account of the distinction between poetry and the novel with the following incisive remarks:

> Poetry expresses the freedom which inheres in man's general timeless unity in society; it is interested in society as the sum and guardian of common instinctive tendencies; it speaks of death, love, hope, sorrow, . . . as all men experience them. The novel is the expression of that freedom which men seek, not in their unity in society but in their differences, of their search for freedom in the pores of society, and therefore of their repulsions from, clashes with and concrete motions against *other* individuals different from themselves.[6]

The novel thus represents change and diversity, poetry changelessness and unity. This distinction makes for their technical differences. Yet they are not mutually exclusive. They both penetrate and enrich reality.

It is the new poets, Caudwell affirms, who must renew experience for us and give us new emotional insights, and attitudes to a new social environment. A poet who brings us both

6. *Ibid.,* p. 208.

to a high degree is a good poet. The content of itself is not the purpose for the poem, but the specific emotional organization directed towards the content. "Poetry soaks external reality—nature and society—with emotional significance."

Thus does poetry continue to speak with a public voice.

I am looking for a meaning of poetry. Caudwell is most convincing indeed. And he writes most persuasively. I take up book after book that purports to show the power and use of poetry. In many ways they confirm Caudwell, and he confirms them. I can of course say, however inadequately, what it does to me. I can also say what I wish it could do. I ponder the various theories about literature, because I suspect that in our practice of poetry in the black world, we are demanding to be assessed by standards that may seem so anti-tradition as to make the critic oriented in the Anglo-Saxon tradition wonder if he should not suspend judgment on black writing—suspend it till there emerges the black aesthetic that is being canvassed at the moment.

There is the theory of literature that sees it as a kind of knowledge—a number of statements leading to a general truth. The statements will often be insights into conduct and its outcome. Fiction becomes a way of arriving at the true conclusions—for example, what happens when an old man becomes doughty enough to ask his daughters to state how much they love him.

We disagree in our moral views because we are not agreed on the facts of a situation which gives rise to such views. A. J. Ayer says in his *Language, Truth and Logic* that we do not try to win a person over to our way of thinking on the moral value of a type action by arguing that his ethical feeling is wrong. We try rather to show that he is wrong about the facts. "If the man has undergone a different process of moral 'conditioning,' we give up trying to win him over by argument."

Laurence Lerner maintains that this cognitive theory helps the literary critic. It enables him to say that the poet produces a "moral effect" by means of insight:

> If the cause of wrong behaviour, or at any rate of wrong opinions, lies in lack of understanding of what a situation is like, then the

> poet (more probably, in this case, the novelist), by clearing away the fog which normally impedes understanding, does at least make it possible for us to see clearly what is the right thing to do. The attraction of this view is that it frees didacticism from exhortation. It is doubtful if exhortation, as such, ever has much effect on anyone; but by this theory it is of no importance, except in so far as the poet himself finds it useful as a way of feeling towards his analysis. It is the analysis itself, the cognitive element, that really matters.[7]

If literature moves readers to moral adjustments by opening their eyes, even if only intellectually, such an effect must derive from the knowledge contained in a work. By working on our feelings, literature can persuade. This knowledge is intuitive, not empirical. Its statements are not verifiable.

Laurence Lerner cites the example of Arthur Miller's dramatic purpose. Miller is not content merely "to show the present countenance" but "to account for what happens." His drama has a moral purpose. Laurence Lerner observes, however, that literature merely as a form of knowledge will not survive. Science also can furnish knowledge, which may supersede the intuitive knowledge inherent in literature. It will have to be something more.

Another theory, that of literature as expression, emerged with the Romantic movement. It produced a revolutionary conception of poetry. The Renaissance idea of a poem as a made thing disappeared, i.e., a thing clear and free of maker. It was easy for lesser poets to strike a "poetic" posture. Its antithesis, the natural, displaced it. "This glorification of the natural, and its equation with the spontaneous, the amorphous, the artless and the personal, is still a potent force in the writing and reading of poetry." [8] A poet imposes his own sensibility on the subject of his poem through imagery, rhythm, ways of feeling that derive from a personal experience. It was the Romantics of the late eighteenth century and early nineteenth century who dis-

7. Laurence Lerner, *The Truest Poetry* (London: Hamish Hamilton, 1960), pp. 7–8. Reprinted by permission of the publisher.

8. Donald Davie, quoted in *ibid.*, p. 34.

covered poetry as an intimate, personal way of dealing with experience. The emphasis with them lay, as it has since lain, on this deeply personal and individualistic manner of feeling the subject, rather than on the latter itself. The historical importance of Wordsworth's "The Prelude" is that the poem rather than its subject (which is actually absent) is a verbal experience, a verbal way of feeling one's capacity for perception grow in one:

> The poem's account of how certain experiences embedded themselves in the poet's mind is also an account of how its own raw material grew: and so is, implicitly, an account of how it came to be written. Its subject is both "the growth of the poet's mind" and also "how that growth grew to clarity in his own mind." [9]

We have thus come to expect to see or feel a close link between a poet's personal experience, his individual sensibility, and his poem. Our emotions lie at the center of our individualism, in a way our ideas do not. A unique sensibility is based on a personal emotion, which makes the poem worth writing. The expression theory rests on this view. One writes a poem for purposes of relief, of unburdening oneself. The Romantic is thus no longer a craftsman (although he still has technique), he starts out to explore his emotions, his goal being the very means of expressing himself. This aim poetry set for itself came to stay. Only, a theory is building up now that should prevent expression from sinking to the level of mere self-indulgence. The feelings must relate to the reader, either in a general way or through a selected channel to which the reader can or must tune in.

This has something to do with a third theory, which emphasizes that feature in literature that refers to rhetoric and what it does to the reader. It is the affective theory. I cannot accept the theory of criticism that a poet should not worry if he fails to express and communicate emotion to the reader; that a poem should be judged as a thing made, that is free of the writer; that it should therefore be judged without reference to the poet's system of beliefs and so on. Senghor and other African poets

9. *Ibid.*, p. 3.

whose poetry exists *because* of the sentiments contained in *négritude,* and who insist that their poetry expresses these sentiments would, by implication, like their poetry to be judged according to whether it is a successful mouthpiece of the ideology.

And yet generally we keep coming back to Tolstoy's words, that art is a human activity by means of which a person carries over to others feelings he has experienced. These others are affected by the feelings and also experience them. If art has to do this successfully, it has to be sincere and accessible to the reader or viewer. Thus only can it be available to a wide public.

I. A. Richards says rightly:

> The very process of getting the work "right" has itself, so far as the artist is normal, immense communicative consequences. . . . It will when "right" have much greater communicative power than it would have if "wrong." The degree to which it accords with the relevant experience of the artist is a measure of the degree to which it will arouse similar experiences in others.[10]

Richards makes this claim after asserting that the artist is not as a rule deliberately and consciously engaged in an effort to communicate. He is busy getting the work "right." He keeps out of his mind such considerations as the acceptance of his work by the public. But this conscious indifference to communication does not imply that the communicative aspect is unimportant. It would only diminish its importance "if we were prepared to admit that only our conscious activities matter." Nor does the reluctance of the artist to consider communication as one of his chief goals, and his refusal to be influenced by a desire to move other people mean that communication is not actually his main object. So often we communicate unconsciously:

> It is certain that no mere careful study of communicative possibilities, together with any desire to communicate, however intense, is ever sufficient without close natural correspondence between the poet's impulses and possible impulses in his reader. All

10. I. A. Richards, *Principles of Literary Criticism* (London: Routledge & Kegan Paul, 1949), p. 27. Reprinted by permission of Routledge & Kegan Paul and Harcourt Brace Jovanovich.

> supremely successful communication involves this correspondence, and no planning can take its place. Nor is the deliberate conscious attempt directed to communication so successful as the unconscious indirect method.[11]

This can be borne out, I think, by the fact that we often respond to certain layers of meaning which the writer may not consciously have been planning for in his work.

Richards's theory upholds the expression of emotion. Communication is thus made possible if the writer intends to be understood by the public in the process of expressing emotion. William Empson, himself a poet as well as a critic, endorses the theory about communication and the artist's relation to it:

> If the poetry is sincere, I feel, you are writing it to find your own balance, even to cure yourself. This sort of poetry cannot worry much about the convenience of the reader, because it has more pressing business in hand; but it aims of course at being a real "expression," an externalization of the conflict into public terms, otherwise it would not work for the writer.[12]

I am still searching. After plowing through critical works, what have I come out with? Was it necessary at all to do this? Why not simply read poetry and make your own judgments? It is simply that I have my own preferences and prejudices. I wanted to find out whether any of these are justified. I am impatient when I am confronted with verse whose language is all in knots, and it is so much agony trying to unravel them that I find my emotions freeze or wilt during such an intellectual exercise. For this reason I surround myself with critical statements about poetry by various authorities; to try to extract some consensus of opinion about the subject. Because I feel that only when I have grasped the basic intention inherent in poetry and what it has been doing for generations can I assess its role in situations of conflict. So I read through some of the poets and critics who have something in common with one another and in some way endorse the theories I have been reminding myself of.

11. *Ibid.*, p. 29.
12. Lerner, *The Truest Poetry*, p. 111.

A poem as a vehicle of emotion motivated by a rational understanding of experience . . . Words and experience as an indivisible whole in the poet's sensibility; his use of evocative words to sharpen his awareness of his ways of feeling so that he can communicate them . . . Poetry as emotion riding on meter . . . As lively feeling of situations and power to express them . . . The poet as the man who feels his images and grasps emotionally rather than logically relationships between things . . . The poet no longer thinks of himself as an alien speaking a lofty language to a small circle of initiates; he sees himself as the great Romantics did, as a man speaking to men in a suffering world . . . All lyrical poetry moves with the throbs of the heart, talking of what the poet sees and feels at a time when suddenly a great dawn breaks upon the senses, setting thought alive . . . Poetry is closer to magic, prayer, prophecy, and myth—more so than to craftwork . . . It is heightened or impassioned speech, setting up in the reader a vibration that corresponds with what the poet felt . . . After the initial impact of the object or idea on thought, the poem is written by memory, desire, love, and hate, daydreams and nightmares—by the whole being . . . Pure cold intelligence does not make a poet, whose thoughts are soaked in feeling . . . The tension between the expression of private vision in a public style—the main condition of creation . . . There is the poet who falls back entirely on personal experience, almost wholly removing the tension between experience and literary (i.e., public) form, but still being able to communicate. . . .

This is what many major poets tell us. Throughout, then, we see a heightened emotion about the subject of a poem; an emotion the poet feels is vital and which he wants to communicate.

II

Now for the poetry I want to examine. I shall not deal with the poetry that has been written as an expression of, and an exhortation for, the return to the cultural essence of blackness in Africa; in other words, the poetry of *négritude*. Especially do

I want to exclude the African theater of *négritude.** First, because it is a derivative kind of *négritude*. Second, it is a dialogue between two selves in the African and only indirectly addressed to Western civilization. It moves on both the personal level and that of a small public—the elite; often so much at the public level that there is a "dissociation of sensibility" between what the poet really feels and thinks and does and what he is urging the public to do. For example, one can remain a Roman Catholic or any other kind of Christian or an autocrat while purporting to instill in the people intellectual independence that should reinstate the most fundamental elements of a living past. Third, which is one of the causes for the second, it is an elite poetry, reflecting a major concern of only that tiny part of the pyramid of African society that is assimilated. It speaks a language that does not touch, because it does not concern, the common man. It is quite true that neo-colonialism is with us, full and strong. But there is a considerably large area of choice for the African. He can revolutionize his educational system, set his own standards, cut loose from Christianity and Islam altogether or liberate them in such a way that they cannot recognize themselves anymore, create a climate for the release of his cultural and creative energies. Culture in Ghana and Nigeria is an eloquent example of how the right choices can promote a release of creative energy. In so much of Africa the black man does not want to choose: he is afraid of seeing his real personality. He does not even realize that he can use modern technology to promote an indigenous culture. Fourth, *négritude* can tell us nothing about how to plan for the second revolution. How can it when it

* In the 1930's, Aimé Césaire, a Negro poet from Martinique, then one of the French colonies in the Caribbean, met Léopold Sédar Senghor of Senegal, and Léon Damas, also Caribbean, in Paris. Césaire used the word *négritude* to mean everything tangible and intangible in the cultural values of the Negro, and the conscious assertion of these. The term came to mean the total sum of Negro values. The African poets took over the concept because they felt it answered their own needs as people so assimilated into French culture that they felt cut off from their African roots. Their poetry, therefore, became an intellectual and emotional projection into pastoral Africa. The American Negroes also went through this phase in the 1920's and 1930's.

never addressed itself to power, even when it was most necessary to do so?

The Senegalese school of *négritude* seldom runs full tilt against white authority as white power. It is concerned with talking to the elite so as to instill in them a sense of self-pride as black people. At the time it began it had a vigorous sense of purpose. It was a two-pronged attack: on the one hand against colonialism as a symbol of white power, and on the other against Western culture as an instrument of colonialism. But the African school became uninterested in radically upsetting European values: it merely taunted them and laughed at them. Because of this French intellectuals, administrators, Catholics, and German scholars sponsored it and indulged it and even fondled the cowries in the rosary of *négritude*. What a fine thing for the white man to be able to go through African doors and handle any African dish without *wanting* to throw up! Yes, *négritude* was content to lie and sprawl in the African sun, laugh and jeer at Western civilization as a way of life, without organizing the mind against it as an instrument of white power. And while this went on, blacks, in some cases the very ones who spoke *négritude,* slipped into positions of power. *Négritude* could not see blacks as healthy, normal, mature human beings to whom power was nothing new, something the white man had brought into Africa.

I am interested in the frontal attack on power and its instruments. Long after we have attained culturally integrated personalities, power will still be a problem. And poetry in such conflict may have something to tell us that will be relevant for all time. Power is something that always sets us on guard against its encroachment. Culture evokes no such negative attitude. It is a continuous flux of human thought and activity. It is always renewing itself, according to the advancement of man's thought, because its conventions are flexible, whereas those of power are generally rigid. When a culture gives birth to power, it recognizes such a child as a monstrosity.

The conflict I am concerned with here is that between power and the underprivileged: a conflict that involves people of all strata and walks of life. The voice of the poet is in a subtle sense also a public voice, as Christopher Caudwell, quoted earlier, so incisively tells us. But the public voice in a poetry that is shaped and defined by conflict, that defines conflict, that is itself a cry against oppression, comes out stridently. Some of it is sheer exhortation, a facile rejection, and therefore is not "memorable speech." And yet it all expresses a deep-felt emotion that is both private and communal. It is "memorable speech," I think, when the very texture, the very driving force of the words, the very diction is a way of feeling, of searching for equilibrium in the subtlest sense of the phrase and of arriving at the most intensive articulation of a people's yearnings.

I deliberately put aside the African theater of *négritude* as derivative. The earlier Caribbean voices of *négritude* that attained the pitch of articulation in Aimé Césaire's *Cahier d'un retour au pays natal* often lashed out against European culture. They had tremendous force even when the poetry was vituperative.

Haiti, the first Negro republic, was occupied by the United States from 1916 until 1934. During the occupation, Haitian poets rose in anger. In 1931 Jean Brierre wrote in his volume *Le Drapeau de demain*:

> Let all the proud mountain tops of the island
> come together
> And together send forth a single roar,
> Which will bring down the filthy servitude,
> For blood is needed to inscribe the rights of the Negro.[13]

Haiti's Philippe Thoby Marcellin wrote angrily in his poem "Sainement" (1927):

> Swearing an eternal scorn for the refinements of Europe,
> I want henceforth to sing of you, revolutions,
> shootings, massacres,

13. *Race and Colour in Caribbean Literature* by G. R. Coulthard, published for the Institute of Race Relations, London, by the Oxford University Press, 1962, p. 81. © Institute of Race Relations, 1962.

sound of cocomacaques on black shoulders,
. . . .
To strip off your classical trimmings
and stand up naked, very savage and very much
the son of slaves
to sing in a new voice the de profundis
of your rotting civilizations.[14]

Another Haitian, Jacques Roumain, wrote a stinging indictment of the Church (1945):

Surprise
Jesus Mary Joseph
when we catch the missionary by the beard
laughing horribly
to teach him in our turn
by kicking his bottom
that our ancestors are not Gauls,
and that we don't give a damn
for a God who,
if he is the father,
well, we, the dirty niggers
it is obvious that we must be his bastard sons,
and it won't help yelling
Jesus Mary Joseph
like an old bladder spilling over with lies.[15]

In the poem "The New Negro Sermon" (1946), Roumain writes:

. . . .
No brothers, comrades,
we shall pray no more
Our revolt rises like the cry of a stormbird over the rotten splashing of the marshes
We shall no longer sing our sad despairing spirituals
Another song shall surge from our hearts
We unfurl our red flags

14. *Ibid.*, pp. 45–46.
15. *Ibid.*, p. 82.

Stained with the blood of our heroes
Under this sign we shall march
Under this sign we march
Up the damned of the earth
Up the prisoners of hunger.[16]

The rich, Pharisees, landowners have brutalized the Negro. The Church induces humility even before the rich; it is wealthy too. Roumain wields phrases from the Bible for his own purpose. He says the Negroes will not forgive the whites, "for they know what they do." Bleeding Christ has been deified. The monasteries make more money from the thirty pieces of silver which they have extracted for betraying Christ.

Martinique's Aimé Césaire was to write later in his *Cahier* (1947):

. . . .
How much blood in my memory, how many
lagoons! They are covered with death's heads.
They are not covered with water-lilies
Lagoons in my memory. No sashes of women on
their banks
My memory is circled with blood. My remembrance
is girdled with corpses!
And the hail of rum-barrels cleverly sprinkling
our ignoble revolts, the swooning of eyes tender
from having swigged fierce liberty.[17]
. . . .

And then:

And I seek for my country not hearts of dates,
But hearts of men who beat the virile blood to enter
the cities of silver by the great trapezoid door,
and my eyes sweep my square kilometers of paternal

16. *Ibid.*, p. 85.

17. Aimé Césaire, *Cahier d'un retour au pays natal* (Paris: Présence Africaine, 1956), pp. 73–75. Translated by Emile Snyder. Reprinted by permission of the publisher.

earth and I number its wounds with a sort of joy
and I heap one on the other like rare species,
and my reckoning is always augmented by
unforeseen mintings of baseness.[18]
. . . .

What makes Césaire's *Cahier* such a truly moving poem is its emotional range. There are in it the excruciating yell against white power, defiance, the cry of alienated man, the declaration of self-pride, the haunting plaintive song of the slave days. He sees his islands as "scars of the waters," "evidence of the wounds," "crumbs," "cheap paper torn upon the waters." Putting these islands together, these "islands unformed," is his challenge.

Paul Niger of Guadeloupe is bitterly sarcastic in the following poem, "Je n'aime pas l'Afrique":

. . . .
Christ redeemed sinful man and built his Church
in Rome
His voice was heard in the desert. The Church on
top of society
and Society on top of the Church, the one carrying
the other
founded civilization where men, docile to the
ancient wisdom
to appease the old gods, not dead,
sacrifice every ten years several million victims
He had forgotten Africa.
But it was noticed that a race (of men?)
still had not paid God its tribute of black blood, they
reminded him
. . . .
So Jesus spread his hands over the curly heads,
and the Negroes were saved.
Not in this world, of course.[19]

18. *Ibid.*, p. 127.
19. Coulthard, *Race and Colour in Caribbean Literature*, p. 51.

This is an idiom that cannot exclude the slave, the squatter, the peasant, the industrial laborer. It can't be the protest of a restricted few. At its best, it is memorable speech. It has an urgency one has become accustomed to in this period of the second Negro Renaissance in America, at a time when the black man is living under semi-military and cultural siege. It is also an urgency to be observed in southern Africa, where the black man is under military siege but can be, as in South Africa, culturally self-sufficient.

Claude McKay went from one situation of conflict (Jamaica) to another (America) in 1912. At this time Negro life was seething with political agitation, trying to move beyond the conventional Paul Laurence Dunbar and white-sponsored Booker T. Washington. Garveyism was stirring. McKay was bringing into the American situation memories of his plantation people in the West Indies: their suffering and endurance and their song. He later wrote of America:

> Although she feeds me bread of bitterness
> And sinks into my throat her tiger's tooth,
> Stealing my breath of life, I will confess
> I love this cultured hell that tests my youth! [20]

He bears no malice or scorn for America, because he hopes for better things for her ahead. He stands before her "as a rebel fronts a king in state." Perhaps here he thinks he has a fighting chance. For him, it is no simple matter of "either . . . or."

Yet McKay does not spare the white man, who is

> a tiger at my throat,
> Drinking my blood as my life ebbs away.[21]

Whatever the white man may do to him, he will never be made to say

20. Claude McKay, *Selected Poems of Claude McKay* (New York: Bookman Associates, 1953), p. 59. Reprinted by permission of Twayne Publishers, Inc.

21. *Ibid.*, p. 47.

that mud
Is bread for Negroes! Never will I yield.

McKay anticipates the present mood in black America that says you have to be black to know what the black experience is. In "The Negro Tragedy," he writes:

It is the Negro's wounds I want to heal
Because I know the keenness of his pain
Only a thorn-crowned Negro and no white
Can penetrate into the Negro's ken.
. . . .
So what I write is urged out of my blood.
There is no white man who could write my book.[22]

For all his race pride and burning words against whites, he had a conventional manner about him. Perhaps he exercised his human pity and religious dignity and calm overmuch, which gave his verse a serene and formalized tone of protest. McKay's style with its formalities is alien to the American soil and still more to the black American idiom, even of the time when he was writing. And it is decorum that robs his diction of the force it could have had. A situation of conflict must need another kind of lyricism, the kind that connects the poet and therefore the reader directly with the experience—indeed, the kind that *is* the experience itself.

I think the kind of ambivalence one finds in McKay's attitude to whites, his human pity, helped shape the kind of verse he wrote, within a set pattern of decorum. He generalized about universal human behavior before he particularized his experience through the medium of the written word. And yet his volumes of poetry show a period of writing output stretching from 1920 to 1940—a period when poetic formalism was being battered about even by the poets of the Negro Renaissance. In his Jamaican dialect verse, decorum struggles with the dialect, constraint with a sense of release that dialect induces. He ignores the white boss and focuses attention on the sweating, suf-

22. *Ibid.*, p. 50.

fering black laborer in order to show the latter's patience and dignity. He had his agonizing moments in trying to reconcile his position as a policeman in Jamaica with his people's underdog situation.

Arthur Drayton, a Trinidadian scholar, writing about McKay says:

> But if McKay were simply a racial poet it would have been a short step, in these new conditions, from his Jamaican verse to bitter race-conscious work. Instead, however, we find for a long time a sober reaction to his new and disturbing environment. However much this new environment was dominated by the race question, it is clear that McKay, like Countee Cullen after him, was determined that the dignity of the poet's calling was not to be sullied. He refused to allow the quality of his reaction as poet to be warped; and equally he refused to allow the quality of his ambitions and status as a human being to be destroyed. All this affected his poetry, and explains the apparent ambivalence in his love-hate relationship with America.[23]

This suggests that the critic in this particular case is convinced that "dignity" is one of the inherent qualities of a poet's calling. If dignity means seriousness of intent or refers to a heightened form of speech, poetry, by the very nature of its form, has it. I think that any other form of dignity, like decorum or the dignity of sentiments, is relatively artificial and put on. And when it becomes the end rather than the means of self-expression, this kind of dignity stifles poetry.

I cannot imagine that Arthur Drayton wants his use of "dignity" to refer to high rank. For this would come dangerously close to assigning to the poet a special and precious role, such as Trinidad's Harold M. Telemaque is doing in his poem "The Poet's Post." The poet's place, Telemaque says, is "by the wide bright bay/Where your lone voice is the light's preserve." His position is "the pure space." As freedom (the island) is

23. Arthur Drayton, "McKay's Human Pity," from Ulli Beier (ed.), *Introduction to African Literature* (Evanston: Northwestern University Press, 1967), p. 84. Reprinted by permission of Northwestern University Press and Longman Group Ltd.

surrounded by water, the poet needs to "search for a land above the sealight,/Find the sky regions clean and immune." [24]

McKay reacted strongly to suffering, conflict. But another man who was also a poet might react similarly but resolve the tension between man and poet differently; between a poet who feels as a man and his effort to express it in public terms.

It is easy to slip into a value judgment between, on the one hand, a poetry that hits the level of local response and at the same time has relevance for the larger world audience and, on the other hand, a poetry that is only or largely local in appeal. The former is often considered to be superior, or "more meaningful." We need not make a value judgment here. Particularly as between two worlds that consider themselves culturally opposed, and when the black world is at least partially in the process of withdrawing from a Western scheme of aesthetic values. It is incidentally for this reason that the aesthetic proposed by Caudwell, Lerner, Richards, and of the practicing poets cited earlier in this essay is one that I deliberately decided to use as a sounding box for the examination of the poetry of revolt under review. It is an aesthetic that is basic to the very existence of poetry, and I do not imagine black poets will disagree radically with it. At this basic level we are all doing the same thing, black or white.

Because McKay sought to resolve his tensions as poet and man the way he did—in generally universal terms (to use the phrase loosely and broadly)—the impact of his poetry on his immediate black audience may have been diminished. It may be that the sonnet form lends the dignity or nobility to the sentiments McKay expresses in his famous "If we must die, let it not be like hogs/Hunted and penned in an inglorious spot." [25]

Gwendolyn Brooks, the Chicago poet, writes much poetry around life in the backyards, kitchenettes, in the streets, in rented backrooms "full of beads and receipts and dolls and cloths, tobacco crumbs, vases and fringes." Every so often when

24. Harold M. Telemaque, "The Poet's Post," *Freedomways,* IV, No. 3 (Summer, 1964), 366. Reprinted by permission of Freedomways Associates.

25. McKay, *Selected Poems of Claude McKay,* p. 36.

we have found ourselves in a relatively privileged position we long to join those in the backyard or in the alleys:

> where it's rough and untended and hungry weed grows
> A girl gets sick of a rose.[26]

There is vitality in the alleys. People are more expressive—those "the middle class calls bad." We want to join them, to

> wear the brave stockings of night-black lace
> And strut down the streets with paint on my face

by way of snapping out of our dead-end existence.

Miss Brooks takes us through scenes where there are broken windows, "hiding their shame with newsprint"; and where you hear "Lonesome Blues, the Long-lost Blues"; "sore avenues" where no Saint-Saëns, no Tchaikovsky or Grieg can be heard. Who could appreciate their music anyhow,

> Since a man must bring
> To music what his mother spanked him for
> When he was two: bits of forgotten hate,
> Devotion: whether or not his mattress hurts?

This has something to do with the assertion of the black Americans: that to sing blues one must have paid the price first —by suffering.

We are presented with vivid scenes, such as that of Satin-Legs Smith flaunting his man-about-town airs on a Sunday:

> The pasts of his ancestors lean against
> Him. Crowd him. Fog out his identity.
> Hundreds of hungers mingle with his own,
> Hundreds of voices advise so dexterously
> He quite considers his reactions his
> Judges he walks most powerfully alone,
> That everything is—simply what it is.

26. This and the following quotations have been taken from Gwendolyn Brooks, *Selected Poems* (New York: Harper & Row, 1963), *passim*. Reprinted by permission of the publisher.

Miss Brooks is essentially a dramatic poet, who is interested in setting and character and movement. So she is interested in those features of her people's life that go to define the setting of conflict, without any direct reference to the conflict itself. She is interested in bringing out in its subtlest nuances the color of life that conflict eventually creates. Her verse teems with words and phrases that represent motion and outward appearance, which in turn lead us to something deeper. Here are some from *Selected Poems*: "fight with fried potatoes" (p. 3); "eased my dim dears at the breast" (p. 4); "I want a peek at the back" (p. 6); "the damp small pulps with a little or with no hair" (i.e., children of a woman who has aborted) (p. 4); "the alley—where the charity children play" (p. 6); "wear the brave stockings of night-black lace" (p. 6); "He wakes, unwinds, elaborately: a cat/Tawny, reluctant, royal" (p. 6 of "Satin-Legs Smith"); "shake hands with paupers" (p. 13); "He dances down the hotel steps that keep/Remnants of last night's high life and distress" (p. 15); "In Queen lace stockings with ambitious heels/that strain to kiss the calves, and vivid shoes" (i.e., of Smith's girl) (p. 17); "Kick the law into their teeth" (p. 19); "Her bacon burned. She/Hastened to hide it in the step-on-can" (p. 75); " 'What I want,' the older baby said,/'is 'lasses on my jam.' Whereupon the younger baby/Picked up the molasses pitcher and threw/The molasses in his brothers' faces" (p. 78).

In the dramatic monologue "Negro Hero" the soldier says he had to kick the white people's law into their teeth in order to be able to fight in their army:

> However I have heard that sometimes you have to deal
> Devilishly with drowning men in order to swim
>   them to shore
> Or they will haul themselves and you to the trash
>   and the fish beneath.

And all for what?—for "their white-gowned democracy"—the "fair lady/With her knife lying cold, straight, in the softness of her sweet-flowing sleeve." So obtuse are they, though, that they must still be asking if his blood is good enough to be spilled for them. Is he clean enough? After all a southern white man can still say:

> "I'd rather be shot in the head
> Or ridden to waste on the back of a flood
> Than saved by the drop of a black man's blood."

The soldier feels satisfied that he has done a good job.

Miss Brooks laughs at those nice women from the Ladies' Betterment League who try to help the poor. It must be "the worthy poor. The very very worthy/And beautiful poor. Perhaps just not too swarthy?" They should not be too dirty or dim. They should be

> something less than derelict or dull.
> Not staunch enough to stab, though, gaze for gaze!

The ladies are visiting the poor settlement when they are repelled by the stench from the urine and garbage, from the smoke, diapers, and those things they call chitterlings; from the general decay. They agree that it will be better to leave and breathe better outside.

> Perhaps the money can be posted.
> Perhaps they two may choose another Slum!
> Some serious sooty half-unhappy home!—
> Where loathe-love likelier may be invested.
> Keeping their scented bodies in the center
> Of the hall as they walk down the hysterical hall,
> They allow their lovely skirts to graze no wall,

—they are off, trying not to inhale the loaded air.

The Mecca Building in Chicago is the scene of several dramatic incidents in Gwendolyn Brooks's long narrative poem, "In the Mecca." [27] The building is a U-shaped apartment block erected in 1891, consisting of 176 units. The courtyard is a

27. This and the following quotations have been taken from Gwendolyn Brooks, *In the Mecca* (New York: Harper & Row, 1964), pp. 5–55 *passim*. Reprinted by permission of the publisher.

squalid enclosure, littered with newspapers, tin cans, milk cartons, and broken glass. The poet captures for us the quality of life here. There is movement right at the opening of the poem. Mrs. Sallie is ascending "the sick and influential stair,"

> Infirm booms
> and suns that have not spoken die behind this
> low-brown butterball.

There is a succession of vivid character sketches throughout the narrative. But the poet breathes life into the characters; like Prophet Williams,

> rich with Bible, pimples, pout: who reeks
> with lust for his disciples, is an engine
> of candid steel hugging combustibles.

Mrs. Sallie's daughter, Pepita, disappears and there is a doleful refrain throughout the rest of the poem to tell us so-and-so has not seen Pepita. When the law comes to the Mecca, "it trots about the Mecca/It pounds a dozen doors."

There are interludes about black poets like Senghor and Don Lee. To read Lee's poem is to get right into the center of the conflict. And the allusion to him here gives us a context for the Mecca:

> Don Lee wants
> not a various America.
> Don Lee wants
> a new nation
> under nothing;
> a physical light that waxes; he does not want to
> be exorcised, adjoining, and revered;
> . . . .
> is not candle lit
> but stands out in the auspices of fire
> and rock and jungle-flail;
> wants
> new art and anthem; will
> want a new music screaming in the sun.

One character, Amos, asks if Negroes are going to sit on themselves, waiting behind roses and veils for monsters to maul them, for bulls to charge on them always. He prays for America:

> Bathe her in her beautiful blood.
> A long blood bath will wash her pure.
> Her skin needs special care.
> Let this good rage continue out beyond
> her power to believe or to surmise.
> Slap the false sweetness from that face
> Great-nailed boots
> must kick her prostrate, heel-grind that
> soft breast,
> outrage her saucy pride,
> remove her fair fine mask
> Let her lie there, panting and wild, her pain
> red, running roughly through the illustrious
> ruin—
> . . . .
> Then shall she rise, recover
> Never to forget.

Yet another character, "Way-out Morgan," collects guns. He is never hungry, he is lean. He thrives on the vision of dead whites. He feeds on the memory of the beating-up he received, of the mob-raping of his sister in Mississippi. As he piles up his guns, he

> listens to Blackness stern and blunt and beautiful,
> organ-rich Blackness telling a terrible story.

His mind is fixed on the day of reckoning, the day of ruin. Conflict, revenge, let America burn and bleed, so that she never forget, so that she be pure.

> Pepita has been murdered, by one of the Mecca
> residents.

How ingeniously Gwendolyn Brooks uses this dramatic form. Within it, always under control, but still with unmistakable clarity, conflict makes its loud report. And yet she never restricts or bullies our responses.

Even in her more contemplative mood, as in the few poems that follow "In the Mecca," the dramatic element persists. The boy who breaks glass during a riot is creating something:

> I shall create! If not a note, a hole.
> If not an overture, a desecration.

The sound of breaking glass is "a cry of art." Always the incentives to violence are "loneliness and fidgety revenge." And the Negro cries against the white man:

> It was you, it was you who threw away my name!
> And this is everything I have for me.

Of Medgar Evers, the civil rights leader who was murdered by Southern whites, Miss Brooks says he "annoyed confetti and assorted brands of businessmen's eyes." She acknowledges that the old constitutional-gradualist methods of struggling for civil rights are worn out, useless:

> Old styles, old tempos, all the engagement of
> the day—the sedate, the regulated fray—
> the antique light, the moral rose, old gusts,
> tight whistlings from the past, the mothballs
> in the love at last our man forswore.

She exhorts, through a persona as always, her people to build their Church. Not with brick, or corten, or granite. But with love, love like the eyes of a lion, love like sunrise, like black, "our black."

She has caught on easily, through her dramatic medium, to the new urgency we see in the younger poets. The result is a powerhouse of feeling coming out through a driving diction.

> This is the urgency: Live!
> and have your blooming in the noise of the
>   whirlwind.

The poet urges her audience to arrest something in the spin of things; to "endorse the splendor splashes" of new poetry; control the diction that is being reduced to utilitarian writing. But they should know that "the whirlwind is our commonwealth." Strife is there. You don't ride it with a facile diction, sweet sonneteering. Nevertheless people must live. Once you acknowledge strife,

> Live and go out
> Define and
> medicate the whirlwind;

and "conduct your blooming in the noise and whip of the whirlwind." Which is what she has herself been capable of. She has a lot to teach us.

The poetry of Samuel Allen (who also uses the name Paul Vesey) also has narrative movement.[28] But he does not try to capture the various facets of an experience as Miss Brooks does in order to build up a picture of conflict. His protagonist is often caught up in situations that reveal his character. Mr. Allen's narrative quivers with the urgency of the chase, the lynching, the castration, "hail of steel," the sirens, rebellion that much of his poetry talks about. Throughout our senses are kept alive to the "unbevelled hammers of pain." You know that his protagonist is also the Negro race. A strong elegiac note comes in often. His most complex poem is the allegorical "The Staircase," of which he writes: "Upon it, as much as any other poem, I would rest my case, I think, and that of the Negro in this land."

The staircase is the rotten, squalid path and dwelling place of the Negro people. It turns and pants with the life that inhabits it. A woman screams from her "den." The protagonist's twin brother—any other black young man—is on the run, and comes

28. The following quotations have been taken from Samuel Allen, *Ivory Tusks and Other Poems* (Millbrook, New York: Poets Press, 1968). This book was printed in a limited edition without page numbers. Reprinted by permission of the author.

up the staircase dogged by that "hail of steel." They gun him down. Death looms large over that staircase: the Negro experience in a nutshell.

The poet, the black man, will always think of the time he was wrenched from his parents, from their love, the day the whites laid their hands on him. It will come back to him like a nightmare, in which "I could not cry out and the cold gray waves/ Came over me O stifling me and drowning me." His reveries will be of

> thicknecked countrymen
> raging to the kill
> their muscles massive
> for a bit of murder.

The lynchee is in reality being anointed. Before he drifts into "death's numbing kingdom," we have witnessed their sacrificial rites, narrated by the poem in vivid searing terms that take the mind back to the ancient days of ritual murder.

Nat Turner has become the symbol of black revolt:

> And I rebel against this fate
> And I will raise a voice against it
> Till the indifferent doomed, till every demon
> Squat in his wet hole,
> Shall pause
> And break from unsmiling cackle
> Into a bloodflecked mounting roar of exultation.

Here, once more, we see the traditional function of the poet. The man who must inspire courage, endurance, rebellion with passionate, memorable speech. How else can you, the poet, see your enemy but as serpents circling from their mounds? How can you be deaf to the "whisper warning shout" riding "down the terrible night"? How can you be insensible of "the dread of the knife and the rope/the Terror of the hissing faggot," of "the sheriff's face huge and high among the trees/riding the vengeful night"?

How can I the reader be left unmoved by the poignant tone

of the poem "My Brother John"? Brother John ridiculed his sister's poems of grief and fear. He could never find his name; he played meek and mild. Then they collected him, hung him up. Obviously hissing menacingly, the sister says, "I *shall* not weep, my brother John!"

Samuel Allen sees the executioner and his associates "ponderous, bloated" tremble with pants wet, eyes wild, neck bulging. Swiftly we are shown "the big house of history," where the executioner lies stretched out, dead:

> Cold on the slab of judgment,
> Felled by his own cold horror
> His last wild glazed unbelieving despair.

And so the river of history sweeps him on and swallows him up, "Red from the mangled host/he sent before." The dramatic method is Samuel Allen's forte. Most of his other verse is cold and passionless.

Elsewhere I make a statement about an African poem, that facile rejection and facile acceptance do not make good poetry. The kind of poetry I have reviewed—by Gwendolyn Brooks and Samuel Allen—has gone beyond the facile, by which I mean a simple-minded, idle, or surface reaction. These poets are speaking the language of most of the 25 million blacks: their sentiments, their revulsion, their revolt, dumb, unspoken, or spoken.

LeRoi Jones's early poetry is difficult. It even found its way into white American anthologies as a token Negro might be found in a white club. And after I have been struggling to decode his knotted language that darts in so many directions, the parentheses that run wild in much of the poetry—all in vain—I have no capacity for an emotional response for even the little I can understand. I feel as if I had been wading through a swamp the extent and shape of which I could not and cannot comprehend. What is often so exasperating about such poetry is that one suspects, and perhaps even *feels,* from the ring of the words that there is a coherent meaning here.

The little I can partially grasp consists of some verses in his

The Dead Lecturer. In the poem "A Contract," the poet feels that in this money-ridden system music, feeling, and speech corrode. The poet fears death for man, for learning, and for himself. The whites live by lies and tell themselves that they have complete mastery over the "stupid niggers." Although any white poet could say the same about a money-ridden society, the line "so complete their mastery, of these stupid niggers" tells us that the poet is speaking as a black man.

The blacks, it seems, are being purged of the illusion that whites are or can be their brothers:

> You are no brothers, dirty woogies, dying under
> dried rinds, in massa's
> droopy tuxedos. Cab Calloways of the soul, at
> the soul's juncture, a
> music, they think will save them from our eyes.[29]

We are reminded here that an oppressor will tell the underdog to sing and dance, even sponsor such an activity and advertise it abroad, and so turn the underdog's attention away from thoughts about oppression. The Babylonians who "carried us away captive required of us a song, and they that wasted us required of us mirth, saying, 'Sing us one of the songs of Zion!' If I forget thee, O Jerusalem, let my right hand forget her cunning." And the poet will not have his tongue "cleave to the roof of his mouth."

LeRoi Jones's shafts are once more aimed at the whites who scream "economics!" while they kill. And what have they to show for it but

> the stink of their failure
> the peacock insolence of zombie regimes
> the diaphanous silence of empty churches
> the mock solitude of a spastic's art.

29. This and the following quotations have been taken from LeRoi Jones, *The Dead Lecturer* (New York: Grove Press, 1964), *passim*. Reprinted by permission of The Sterling Lord Agency, Inc. © 1964 by LeRoi Jones.

He goes against the "shabby personalities," against the homosexual who fancies he's being anarchist when he speaks out against Elk-Sundays in towns that are quieter than his, against the music of these shabby personalities, their lunches, their "afternoon spas/with telephone booths, butterflies, grayhaired anonymous trustees/dying with the afternoon."

A powerful statement is "Green Lantern's Solo." Jones is accessible here; the language opens up as it were. "Murder is speaking of us," the poet says, breaking, running, hiding. He is surrounded by "the smelly ghosts of wounded intellectuals," harassed by their "mysterious jungle." There is sterility everywhere: lyric poets think they can produce poetry without ever having experienced orgasm, i.e., having delved deep into experience and suffered, without having loved and felt things like sex till one was cloyed.

"The completely free are the completely innocent," and a black man cannot claim this—in spite of words that are bandied about from city to city, in spite of words about love, in spite of brilliant men like Marx and Rousseau who were stupid enough to think the world would want to learn from their wisdom and to change. All we have is ourselves—lovers, heroes, disgustingly evil creatures, conducting a dialogue with our selves, exchanging roles. Life sprawls to take in all "the islands of mankind," to take in all commerce, beauty, lust. What one thinks represents what all men think. Truth and lie are not absolutes: they exist as such only in the naïve mind of a fool. A mind that creates the idea of one mind, or right or God—an absolute overseeing Idea which turns out to be a doctrinaire system by which we measure the profit and loss of the soul.

Much of LeRoi Jones's poetry is about both the black experience and that of man in general. The mood switches from statements about or probings into the general condition of man, as a glance at even my poor paraphrase will show. He says elsewhere in "Green Lantern's Solo" that even "the floating strangeness of the poet's mind" is not free. It is a case of the intellect reshaping, renaming, defining experience which must then be subjected to the rigorous discipline of art. Things then are fixed; or they shift according only as we see them and feel them or master them. One feels LeRoi Jones says this because his poetry is art and craft in a sense that lesser verse is not. And he wants it to be art as well as a statement.

Also, he is convinced of the importance of poetry (*lyric,* as he puts it). In "A Guerrilla Handbook" he seems to say that just as a seed will not grow on a palm, a hand grenade or rifle in the guerrilla's hand brings destruction. If tree trunks in their strength and justification are socialists, they cannot be held responsible if their affiliates, i.e., the leaves, make noise, dry up, and are blown to the sea. So maybe the guerrilla cannot be blamed if he destroys: he does so in order to build. We can imagine "silent political rain against the speech of friends" to refer to underground politics against the background of people's talk, including the poet's. The poet is to be loved: he is trapped; he has no escape route except as it were to "write himself out" of the trap. The guerrilla must "convince the living that the dead cannot sing." Being trapped is like being dead, and the prisoner cannot sing. Being physically dead, one cannot sing, so the guerrilla must remove autocratic rule that holds the sentence of death over everybody who rebels.

LeRoi Jones is concerned that, as a lecturer substituting a dead one, he has nothing to offer the poor. Whatever he will reveal in his lectures must be ugly, or else fanciful ideas. But if the poor, whom "cold air batters," whose "minds turn open like sores," need life, they should at least be fed. It is only out of vanity that he has become a poet and a lecturer. All he can boast is "a simple muttering elegance":

> And I am frightened
> that the flame of my sickness
> will burn off my face. And leave
> the bones, my stewed black skull,
> an empty cage of failure.

That will be when he is no longer black, having been bleached by the wrong pursuits. And yet must a black man stop teaching and writing because he does not cater to the material needs of the poor? Is the "teacher" a charlatan simply because

> big birds will run off from their young
> if they follow too closely;

or because

> the drowned youths at puberty
> . . . did not allow that ritual
> was stronger than
> their mother's breasts?

All the same the despair, as a black experience, is an agony of a different kind and intensity from that in white people among *their* poor. Jones's final answer is in his social essays titled *Home*:

> My faith in Melville, for instance, and the faith I give his language is completely passed through the world into my own references of mind and spirit. They cannot be got at. But I work with street people on picketing and lecturing poor, ignorant Negroes because that work is not only necessary, but open to any interpretation. It passes too, beyond results, to where I feel the use of anything.[30]

I speak of LeRoi Jones's difficulty or inaccessibility in much of *The Dead Lecturer*. He is often as difficult as the late Christopher Okigbo, whose *Heavensgate* poems he says are much more "literary" than John Pepper Clark's work: "It suffers from that quality, which seems to make it less an extension of Mr. Okigbo's qua himself than it is a reflection of an ambitious social/aesthetic program." [31] In this matter of erudite and elaborate allusions, I lump Okigbo together with T. S. Eliot and another black American, the late Melvin Tolson. Okigbo handles the music of the English language with remarkable adroitness, and yet his rhythm and sound seldom penetrate the blood,

30. LeRoi Jones, *Home: Social Essays* (New York: William Morrow, 1966), p. 119. Copyright © 1963 by LeRoi Jones. Reprinted by permission of the publisher.

31. *Ibid.*, p. 130.

to use D. H. Lawrence's words about a friend's verse. By the time I have done research into Eliot's and Tolson's allusions, my emotional potential has been dissipated. Kofi Awoonor and Gabriel Okara are fine examples of the poet that penetrates the blood. Jones makes an incisive statement about this matter of communication in his poem "Titles." [32]

His head is "in a fine tangle," he says. He has many lyrics that will not be understood. But

> It is not as if
> there were
> any more beautiful
> way,

than saying things with poetry. Telling me, the reader, that a lyric is going to be difficult does not help me to understand it. But I know, from reading those poems I *do* understand and which therefore move me, I am prepared to take my chances with Jones and read him several times over. It is not a matter of allusions with him: it is another kind of intellectual complexity. He knows too that he is taking his chances when he writes a kind of poetry that several others besides me will not take the trouble to reread. If I were not teaching poetry, and were not also interested in black poetry in America, I do not think I should take so much trouble. Maybe he will say that's the people he writes for—those who are interested desperately enough. That is still taking a chance. Every so often I am happy to understand a poem of his. Because I find it is rich, it says a hell of a lot, it penetrates the blood. But I don't want to feel, as the old Browning Society used to feel, I belong to a coterie—the chosen ones who can enter LeRoi Jones's mental and spiritual workshop. I want to be able to shout and slap the back of a friend, shake him up and scream, *This is poetry, man!* and get a similar reaction from him.

In criticizing the earlier poetry of the Negro, LeRoi Jones says it tells us that the black man has been oppressed, misused

32. Jones, *The Dead Lecturer*, p. 34.

by the white man. Very few of them say what it is like to be oppressed. We are faced with the act of protest, he adds: a gun, a picket sign, would be more useful:

> I mean there is no point in this being poetry *especially*. No poetic point has been made. . . . [T]he reason there have not been a great many interesting Negro writers (in the U.S.) is that most of the Negroes who've found themselves in a position to become writers were middle class Negroes who thought of literature as a way of proving they were not "inferior." . . . But let there be no misunderstanding. I do believe, desperately, in a "poetry of ideas." Poems have got, literally, to be about something. And the weights of love, murder, history, economics, etc. have got to drag whoever's writing in a personally sanctified direction or there will be no poems at all. But it is not the direction that's interesting or makes literature or art, but the replaying of it by the poet. All of my work, for instance, is written by a Negro writer. If I say, "Look at that woman falling out of the window," it is a Negro who is saying it, . . . and that fact should *somehow* inform the telling. . . . It should inform through the intensity of personal response and the uniqueness of private emotional concern. A poet writing a poem about the black man being oppressed by the white must keep that concern *within* the poem. Otherwise there will form a hardshell of talk and opinion around what the poet thinks he is saying, and the matter will be lost. . . . We are stung by some things in our lives that must tell who we are, almost as specifically as on our driver's license. . . . They comprise an effortless power readily at our use if we can find an effective method. Which is what I mean if I ever say the word "technique"; how to effectively express what we know.[33]

All these things, of course, bounce back to the poetics I surveyed at the beginning of this essay. All serious poets will tell you that they aim at presenting experience effectively, with a "personal intensity," and in terms of a *unique private emotion*. LeRoi Jones goes a bit further in his insistence that the black experience will be different; black art will have a built-in concern with the Negro's plight as an underdog; it will be informed

33. Jones, *Home: Social Essays*, pp. 122–124.

by the fact that it is a *Negro* that is feeling it and expressing himself.

When LeRoi Jones's tone changes to that of a man of action, which he often is, his language opens up, stretches out, as it were, and he is easy to understand without losing his force, except when it is pure exhortation. "Short Speech to My Friends" begins:

> A political art, let it be
> tenderness, low strings the fingers
> touch, or the width of autumn
> climbing wider avenues, among the virtue
> and dignity of knowing what city
> you're in, who to talk to, what clothes
> —even what buttons—to wear. I address
> the society
> the image, of
> common utopia.[34]

The black man has tried for years to enter the white man's kingdoms. The blues become the black man's tears issuing out of poor homes. It is poverty that makes the Negro's music, poetry, drama, and so on. So here morality and humanity combine.

Oppression, conflict, create heroes of their own kind. There is the literary man; another hero apes the white man's errors and arrogance; there are the trucker, boxer, valet, bartender who exchange roles. There are pretentious heroes who are now dead from heat exhaustion as they roam the beach in typical middle-class fashion. What to do? Silence may be the answer: even literacy won't do. Let the spit one aimed at the intellectual freeze midair.

One is reminded of D. H. Lawrence's description of what poetry is like today—"stark, bare, rocky directness of statement" —when one reads some of the newer verse of LeRoi Jones. Some of this was quoted against him by the judge at his trial following upon the July riots in Newark, New Jersey.

34. Jones, *The Dead Lecturer*, p. 29.

The poem "Black People" is pure exhortation. It does not make memorable speech. But then Jones means it to be a thing for the present, for *now*. The reader is not meant even to be disturbed: there is no time for that: he is expected to have been already disturbed by the time these words reach him:

> . . . Smash the window at night (these are magic
> actions) smash the windows daytime, anytime,
> together, let's smash the window drag the shit
> from in there. No money down. No time to
> pay. Just take what you want. The magic dance
> in the street. Run up and down Broad Street
> niggers, take the shit you want. Take their
> lives if need be, but get what you want what
> you need. Dance up and down the streets,
> turn all the music up, run through the streets
> with music, beautiful radios on Market Street,
> they are brought here especially for you. Our
> brothers are moving all over, smashing at
> jellywhite faces. We must make our own World
> man, our own world, and we can not do this unless
> the white man is dead . . .[35]

We may even regard this passage as an anti-poem. There is no need to prove why it does not make memorable speech, such as we associate with true poetry.

"The Black Man Is Making New Gods"[36] can easily be read as an anti-Semitic piece. There is the Jew who looks and acts desperately atheist, who is eager to identify with the "poor" blacks, work with them, and then skulk when things get too hot. He is then ripe to sell out. Jones has had plenty of experience with this kind of Jew. There is the other Jew who allowed himself to be nailed to the cross, whom other whites deified for us to worship. There is the Jew who makes his money. The black man is chained to all these images. They are false gods.

35. LeRoi Jones, "Black People," *Evergreen Review*, No. 50 (December, 1967), p. 49. Reprinted by permission of The Sterling Lord Agency.
36. *Ibid.*, p. 49.

Even the Jew who died in the Nazi furnaces is said to be involved in the betrayal. Perhaps we thought that as the Jews suffered so much under the Nazis, their people should identify with oppressed humanity in America, indeed all over the world. But now even what they went to the gas chambers and the furnaces for does not seem to matter to Jones. And this in turn is intended to diminish our image of the 6 million: those mass killings, Jones would say, don't matter anymore. We live with robots and may become them too, "serving their dirty image." In Jones's words they are "little dirty bastards/talking arithmetic they sucked from the arab's/head." He threatens murder, beatings-up—"the best yet to come." When he is done with them, their bodies will be relegated to a cold box labeled "Dangerous Germ Culture."

A man's life often writes his poem and shapes it. LeRoi Jones lives his poetry. This fighting, murderous talk is the language of everyday speech. It is exhortation also. It expresses and conveys the poet's anger with which a particular audience is expected to identify. The poet represents here the Jew in a historical context that is quite clear to us: we are looking at the Jew whose people have just experienced a holocaust in Germany. So he is not just a vague representation of the white American. Somewhere along the line of thought in this poem I get confused. The Jews ordered Jesus to be hanged. Two thousand years later millions of them end up in the Nazi gas chambers and ovens. I find it difficult to understand who the villains are at any time. Who is the black holy ghost? Is he one of Jones's Christian hangups?

We are still at the level of revolt in this poem. If we are to attach any significance to its title, it must be that the poet wants us to think about the new gods the black man is making, something one can only read between the lines. But only the need to make them is implied, not *what* gods they are or should be. The Christian God is indeed indifferent to the black man's suffering: according to the Calvinists, He must be even mean. If you painted Christ black you'd still have to pull yourself out of the mire. There is a hollowness in the miles and miles of words that are being written about the Christian God. But by and large the black man means to keep the faith or else switches over to the Mohammedan god, who does not temper the winds for the shorn lamb either; or he remains a humanist, atheist, or agnostic. These factors have every bit to do with the new gods we are said to be making. Yes, it certainly behooves us to pause and ponder and question beliefs that have been burnt into our minds. And Jones's poem makes us do this. There is a diction, such as we find in the poem, that hits the reader on the head as it were, with a bludgeoning effect. There is the other kind Jones writes, in which thoughts and feelings are distilled slowly and calmly like water filtering through sand. There is beauty and a profound sense of veneration in the poem "leroy." [37] It is an image of his mother, sitting sad in the yard, looking

> into the future of the soul.

There are black angels hovering over her, carrying the life of the ancestors "and knowledge, and the strong nigger feeling." He feels hypnotized when he sees her picture in the yearbook, with memories of those many years ago

> from that vantage of knowledge passed
> on to her passed on
> to me and all the other black people of our time.

And then the last powerful lines that assert his sense of mission:

> When I die, the consciousness I carry I will to
> black people. May they pick me apart
> and take the
> useful parts, the sweet meat of my feelings
> and leave
> the bitter bullshit rotten white parts alone.

In a foreword to his collection of poems *Black Magic Poetry,* LeRoi Jones confesses to a kind of progression in his career as

37. *Ibid.,* p. 48.

a poet. In the section of poetry headed "Sabotage" (1961–63), the poet purports to be recognizing the "superstructure of filth Americans call their way of life, and (wanting) to see it fall." The section labeled "Target Study" (1963–65) means, he says, that he is reconnoitering, as it were, the cities that the bomber is soon to destroy. He claims that he is less passive at this stage, less "literary" in a useless way. And then the "Black Art" section (1965–66) purports to produce the final devastating thrust and to inspire the will to build.

Jones makes it quite clear in the foreword his conviction that, unlike in the days of "suicide notes" and "dead lecturers," he is now connecting "the most beautiful part of himself to the black people." He sounds the ideal of a "whole race connected in its darkness, in its sweetness." I cannot imagine that even the poetry just referred to can be understood by any but the enlightened, the highly literate. Take for instance a readily accessible poem like "Sisters in the Fog" appearing together with the somber "leroy" in the "Black Art" section:

> The rewards of love
> are multifaced. They'll change
> you are changed and worn and real.
> So the spikes of sun wont kill you
> if you're wrong, grow old in the ease
> of your brothers blood, and be plain dumb niggers
> with the only quality truly transferable among humans,
> stupidity. There are fights in the streets with the cops
> and a brother is wounded and jailed. His wife
> screams curses
> at life, the time, the motion, god, all beauty,
> and her wounded
> self. Would that that self would disappear and she grow
> more beautiful
> than the fake virgin of the christians, Mary Marvel, whose
> antics invented
> cuckoldry as hip in the sacred texts of the beasts. Would
> that we would

all become what the dream of reality insists we
    can become.[38]

An incisive statement, all in all. But consider the imagery in "the rewards of love are multifaced"; "the spikes of sun"; "grow old in the ease of your brothers blood"; "his wife screams curses at life, the time, the motion, god, all beauty, and her wounded self"; "sacred texts of the beasts"; "the dream of reality." Vivid and effective imagery, justly reflecting the cruelty of the times. To be able to build up a coherent picture in the mind, as the sum total of the suggestions that are sparked off by the images, the reader needs to be educated. You simply could not confront a person who has not reached at least twelfth grade with this poem and expect him to penetrate its language. Poetry of this kind is a language. It requires an educated mind, sensory perception that operates via rhetoric or the written word, and an understanding of rhetoric that in turn arouses emotions. This kind of poem can only "speak" to a select group of people even though it purports to appeal to the emotions of people who live amid all those fights in the streets with the cops and brothers who are wounded and jailed. People must be taught to read and interpret the language of consciously composed poetry (as distinct from the oral) in the same way as they need to be taught to read and interpret the language of music if they are ever going to appreciate fully what it is all about—a combination of mind, feeling, and language. And LeRoi Jones need not feel guilty or apologize for it. Those people who are close to the core of reality, who feel life at its most basic levels, have their own poetry. They have their own metaphor or symbolism. In the final count their poetry will lead us to the same goal LeRoi would set for us. But they will not express their experience in such terms as "multifaced rewards of love," "spikes of sun," etc. Do we indeed *feel* the language of these people? Certainly we used to live that kind of life, so it should be easy for

38. From *Black Magic Poetry 1961–1967*. Copyright © 1969 by LeRoi Jones. Reprinted by permission of the publisher, The Bobbs-Merrill Company, Inc., the author, and the Ronald Hobbs Literary Agency.

us to connect. Can we rope it into our poetry—the poetry we want to compose and publish? Maybe we can use the idiom or bits of it. As long as the poet is aware that he will be rendering *his* individual state of mind which ties up with the collective consciousness of his people.

The more I read poetry that deliberately uses the speech rhythms and diction of the street or marketplace, the more I am persuaded that it is better spoken than read. This might start a recording industry that has every chance of flourishing and succeeding in speaking directly to a people. Otherwise it has to be printed expressly for the purpose of performing it in small intimate groups. Examples are poetry like that in Don L. Lee's collection *Don't Cry, Scream,* Nikki Giovanni's poems, and some of Larry Neal's, like "Can You Dig It?":

> Can you dig it?
> swinging inshallah
> our spirits cutting through
> the dead West
> in Allah, the word-flesh and spiraling cosmos
> (give it to me baby
> everything is everything)
> in Allah, the spiraling cosmos
> and you blues and black stars
> and you blues, and jamming, and jamming
> nigger sharp rhythms
> into the funky universe,
> can you dig it momma, the magic of these
> mellow voices moaning
> of yester loves and kisses,
> smokey robinson's voice hugs close,
> clinging soggy wet to your body
> the voice slow grinding in the blue corner.
> love haunts and is wet and juice-filled,
> night wife . . .[39]

39. Larry Neal, "Can You Dig It?" *Negro Digest* (September, 1969), p. 81. Reprinted by permission of *Black World.*

I say this also because I have heard these three poets read their verse. The inflection of the voice, the cadence are all part of the performance which is the only reason why the verse was composed. The oral performance of verse has been magnificently exploited by East Wind Associates in New York, who cut a disc called *The Last Poets*. Three black American poets are presented here. There are lead voices and choral responses for each of the thirteen items of verse.

Again, after viewing the superb performance of Ruby Dee and Ossie Davis on television, in which they read Langston Hughes's verse, it is more evident to me than ever before how very little of Hughes's verse could stand without the support of the human voice. This is the language Hughes chose for himself, and he was faithful to it till the end of his days. You take him or leave him on this understanding. Arna Bontemps, on the other hand (to mention only one other major product of the Harlem Renaissance), took a separate road. His passionate intensity is of a kind that is built into the diction and structure of his poem. Hughes was intellectually lightweight, and had a very limited capacity for the passionate rendering of sensuous impressions. There is no special way in which we could say Bontemps' poetry needs the support of the human voice to lend it intensity of feeling.

Larry Neal is for me the most skillful artist among those who adhere to the Black Arts Movement: a man who can combine sound and sense even on the printed page. Even while his verse speaks with the directness of everyday language, as written poetry it holds you with its driving diction and imagery, its staccato movement. Sometimes the words seem to come tumbling down a hill, giving you one jolt after another. His "Orishas" tells us Coltrane's sound "weaves, tearing slowly beating hearts"; it makes "pale things fall dead" or "scurry like rats for the sewer caves"; the sound needs to do something to the Negroes, who are mere "fleshless movements in the funky hallways." Coltrane's sound merges with the voice of Shango (the Yoruba god). The memory of the late jazz musician impels the poet to ask:

Who are the dead?
who are the long list of names in the oceans
who are the figures standing in the cabin doors
as the train highballs North
Who are the wailing children,
bodies ripped into bits of flesh?
I catch aspects of their profiles,
am wound around them like a serpent
grasping for life.
Whose eyes are these, gouged out
mucus smeared in the red earth,
figure hanging tarred above the lynch fire?
what bodies are these crushed and maimed,
or brains kicked out on the piss pavements
of the cities?
How many aspects of truth do you need Negro leaders?
How many angles are there to any story? [40]

As the questions continue in quick succession, we feel we are again listening to an oral performance. Larry Neal keeps pushing, driving, pressing, and ripping his way through to us in "Can I Tell This Story, Or Will You Send Me through All Kinds of Changes?"—

and all we wanted
to do was sing.[41]

Another poetry that is best suited for the oral performance is illustrated by Calvin C. Hernton's "Jitterbugging in the Streets."[42] It is documentary verse that piles on images that evoke the sounds of rioting. It is a whole catalogue of events. But the impact of the piece is cumulative. We shall need to ask

40. From Clarence Major (ed.), *The New Black Poetry* (New York: International Publishers, 1969), p. 93.

41. Larry Neal, "Can I Tell This Story, Or Will You Send Me through All Kinds of Changes?" *Black World* (September, 1970), pp. 54–57. Reprinted by permission of *Black World*.

42. LeRoi Jones and Larry Neal (eds.), *Black Fire: An Anthology of Afro-American Writing* (New York: William Morrow, 1968), p. 210.

of such verse how much of it is documentary and how much represents a search for the *meaning* of a particular experience in the context of the American society. This latter element is at the center of what makes poetry vibrate as a language of its own, beyond the local experience. Lines like the following, from Hernton's "A Black Stick with a Ball of Cotton for a Head . . . ," must certainly vibrate without the orchestration of sounds, sights, and smells of the "Jitterbug" poem:

> Will it be like this, Charlie
> In life's other solidified enterprise?
> Stiff in the strut of the dead
> Bituminous shirt,
> Carbonic boots and spider web,
> Cling to our flesh more fierce
> Than instinct.
> We are a stampede of late supplicants
> Who have found no love in swaddling clothes
> But the mummy of a worthless radiator
> In a cold tenement . . .[43]

These poets are much more accessible than LeRoi Jones even in the more recent poetry for which he claims the quality of a direct impact. And yet he is no inferior poet. Indeed, Jones has had a wider and deeper and even more agonizing experience in trying to reconcile his highly individual intellectual life (if there are any degrees in one's intellectual individualism) with his craft as a poet and its role in his scheme of communication with the public. He simply cannot with honesty claim that he is being read and understood by the man in the street. This man has his own language, which is not Jones's. And the poet is still the prisoner of his intellect.

If, as I believe, black American theater has the best chance and possibilities of evolving an aesthetic of its own, distinct from white American theater, Jones's plays would seem to have

43. Copyright © 1968 by Calvin Hernton. Reprinted from *Black Fire* by LeRoi Jones and Larry Neal. William Morrow & Co., New York, New York. Used with permission of the author and the Ronald Hobbs Literary Agency.

this potentiality rather than his poetry as far as 1966. And yet the symbolism of *Dutchman* is not uniquely black in anything concerning form, although it involves the black experience. And it is certainly not obvious or readily "available" to the unlettered Negro. Indeed Jones packs his plays with the energy of his poetry. At the center of these plays lies the poetic consciousness. *The Slave* and *Toilet* are probably more "available," but only superficially so. It seems to me that a truly black theater will have to come out of the experiments of the New Lafayette. The play will need to be written by the life of the people and hammered out independently of the proscenium arch structure. Africa is doing this today. And yet, assessed on the basis of their conception and for the kind of theater they are intended, *Dutchman, The Slave,* and *Toilet* are intensely moving and well written. We don't have to accept them as indigenously black theater before they can do this to us. They are also a credit to Jones's versatility, intellectual alertness, seriousness of purpose, and inner vitality as a writer. Barring the obscurities and contortions of his earliest poetry, he does not have to believe that his poetry speaks the language of the streets for him to write a good moving poem, the kind we see in his *Black Magic Poetry*.

One would think that if an individual wanted to be heard by everybody, he would naturally speak prose. There must be a reason why a man would choose verse for communicating with a public, a medium we do not speak in our everyday life. Such a preference must have something to do with aesthetics, with the idea of importance and gravity and of memorable speech traditionally associated with poetry. Black poets speak in different keys. And the sociopolitical patterns of black life are so fluid that it becomes absurd to lay down or prescribe styles in absolute terms for such a variable as the distances between writer and audience. The language of poetry speaks to different kinds of people at different times.

For instance, Audre Lorde and Lucille Clifton write beautiful poetry. Theirs are subdued voices: no finger-snapping with-it-ness about their tone. Here are the opening lines of a vivid portrait of Miss Rosie in the poem of that name by Lucille Clifton, taken from her volume *Good Times*:

> When I watch you
> wrapped up like garbage
> sitting, surrounded by the smell
> of too old potato peels
> or
> when I watch you
> in your old man's shoes
> with the little toe cut out
> sitting, waiting for your mind
> like next week's grocery
> I say
> when I watch you
> you wet brown bag of a woman . . .[44]

And these lines from Audre Lorde's "Coal":

> . . . Some words are open
> Like a diamond on glass windows
>   Singing out within the crash the sun
>   makes passing through.
> There are words like stapled chances
> In a perforated book—buy and sign and tear apart—
> And come what wills all chances
> The stub remains
> An ill-pulled tooth with a ragged edge.
> Some words live in my throat
> Breeding like adders. Others
> Know sun, seeking like gypsies over my tongue
> To explode through my lips
> Like young sparrows bursting from shell
> Some words
> Bedevil me.[45]

44. From Lucille Clifton, *Good Times* (New York: Random House, 1969), p. 5. Copyright © 1969 by Lucille Clifton. Reprinted by permission of Random House, Inc.

45. From Audre Lorde, *The First Cities* (New York: Poets Press, 1968), p. 8. Reprinted by permission of the author.

Whatever the key, whatever the diction, there is always the problem of maintaining a delicate balance between the state of mind you want to express as an experience on the one hand and the mysteriously felt sense of urgency and need to speak to someone or to some people on the other.

Although *négritude* anticipated the struggle for political independence in some parts of Africa, the latter left *négritude* far behind. Politics did not need a cultural self-assertion. And after all, only a small segment of the elite was composed of assimilated gentlemen. Again, Africans are not culturally besieged in a way that black Americans are. The siege that apartheid imposed on black South Africans produced peculiar results. At first the blacks assimilated much of European culture with its education. When the ghettos were consolidated by harsher laws, the blacks in turn consolidated their urban culture, thus creating their own music, dance, and communal life at once new, indigenous, and virulent, although politically insecure. Something so many whites would like to share, in spite of themselves, because their own culture is still part of their import trade, an item in their balance of payments. Bantustans (those areas the white ruling class dream of as segregated homelands for the Africans) will freeze cultural mobility, literature will continue to be harassed by the censorship law. But urban culture will continue to create its own innovations.

Being thus besieged and outnumbered, the American Negro has to try to operate on all planes in all areas at the same time. His sense of urgency tells him that the culture bit can push the political and economic machine faster in his own favor. It is not surprising to see a sizable young and virile crop of black poets today invoking the sense of black pride and beauty among their immediate audience. This is all part of the great withdrawal from white standards in various areas of life.

A highly productive poet is Don L. Lee. In his first volume of verse, *Think Black,*[46] he teases and whips up the black con-

46. Don L. Lee, *Think Black* (Detroit: Broadside Press, 1967). Reprinted by permission of the publisher.

sciousness. He regrets the education he got in early life: he was taught to be polite, deceitful, to accept segregation, to grab. "The mistake was made in teaching me/How not to be BLACK."

Irish, Italians, German-Americans can assimilate; even Jews. But not the black: he cannot anyhow, because he is threatened with annihilation.

In his second volume of verse, *Black Pride,*[47] Lee contemplates his shadow, its darkness: how beautiful it is, "with the sun as its lover." Lee is fair-complexioned. In "The Self-Hatred of Don L. Lee"[48] he tells us that at one time he loved his color—

> it
> opened sMall
> doors of
> tokenism
> &
> acceptance.

Then he read Du Bois, Richard Wright, Alain Locke who talk inclusively about "us," "we," and self-awareness as blacks. That is how his "blindness" was "vanquished." He began then to hate his light brown exterior, to love his "inner self which is all black." We are back again, with Don Lee, to the ironic thing that happens when blacks try to tell us Christ was black. Lee's cynicism is quite pointed and devastating in "The Black Christ":

> Off one god
> can't get hooked
> on another elija
> . . . .
> History repeats
> itself ask
> st malcolm

47. Don L. Lee, *Black Pride* (Detroit: Broadside Press, 1968), p. 19. Reprinted by permission of the publisher.
48. *Ibid.*, p. 19.

all because j.c.
was a nigger.[49]

The black man has carried his cross too long, and it is not elevating to any race that it has accumulated martyrs.

In "Contradiction in Essence," [50] Lee says how he met a part-time revolutionist rigged up in African dress, wearing a "natural," always angry, in a hurry, talking black but sleeping white. The theme recurs elsewhere: "Love can be a reality/thru blackness and other colours dark." Watch the Negroes with white minds: they are enemies of black people, "denying self." [51] Some try to come back to us—and we should be glad of it. That is the poem for black minds.

In "Two Poems," [52] Don Lee admits:

i ain't seen no poems stop a .38
i ain't seen no stanzas brake a honkie's head,
i ain't seen no metaphors stop a tank,
i ain't seen no words kill
& if the word was mightier than the sword
pushkin wouldn't be fertilizing russian soil/
& until my similes can protect me from a night
 stick
i guess i'll keep my razor
& buy me some more bullets.

It is also an admission that he does not see poetry ever taking the place of a gun or stopping it. Another statement of the contradictions in the poet's art and role: he keeps writing out of that inner compulsion even if his verse does not immediately change anything. Just like talking, a common human activity. The poet *must* talk, like the Ancient Mariner. His only justification lies in the communal consciousness that he represents and is shaped by. To know ourselves is to know how weak and strong

49. *Ibid.*, p. 23.
50. *Ibid.*, p. 22.
51. *Ibid.*, p. 29.
52. *Ibid.*, p. 13.

and ugly and beautiful we are. This cumulative knowledge of ourselves contributed to by all meaningful and relevant poetry, wherever it comes from, should become a ritual. As in the harvest or funeral or circumcision ritual, we can dramatize our emotions, reaffirm our beliefs and ideals, even revitalize our experiences. The tension between the poet's tendency to break down or dispel myths and the communal urge to make myths that will in turn be reaffirmed through the ritual of poetry—this tension is what the technique of communication is all about. The ritual is not likely to be realized as long as poets become wrapped up in their private concerns to the exclusion of their public. And by and large the new Negro Renaissance, like the African Renaissance, cannot be said to be guilty of this. Larry Neal says, "Essentially, art is relevant when it makes you stronger. That is, the only thing which is fundamental to good art is its ritual quality."

Don Lee hints as much about the ritual essence in poetry when, of the late Langston Hughes, he writes:

> Bravery is that
> little black man
> over there
> surrounded by people
> he's talking . . .
> bravery lies in his
> words,
> he's telling the
> truth
> they say
> he's
> a
> poet.[53]

One of the most powerful poems by Don Lee is "The Death Dance."[54] It ranges over a number of moods and voice inflec-

53. *Ibid.*, p. 17.
54. *Ibid.*, p. 31.

tions. The dance begins with "empty steps," then to "a hip be-bop beat," to tap dancing. Then, as he grows in consciousness, the African ballet becomes his guide. Now he has begun to do "dangerous steps/warriors' steps," in rhythm with all his black brothers:

> & you could hear the cracking of
> gunshots in them & we said that,
> "we were men, black men."

The white man won't like this—seeing him come without being able to stop him. The white man can't possibly mistake the new dance for entertainment:

> you know,
> that when i dance again
> it will be the
> Death Dance

Interwoven in the account of his coming into consciousness is the story of his mother. The woman who slaves for her children, endures humiliation at the hands of white folk, but keeps urging, "son you is a man, a black man."

Lee's latest book of poems (to date), *Don't Cry, Scream,* is not easy to talk *about.* It is a poetry to be spoken, not read silently, otherwise it loses almost all its force. The human voice can integrate the various signs that may mean nothing to the eye except puzzle it. This was confirmed in my mind when I heard Don Lee read publicly from this volume at Columbia University in May, 1969. There is little more one can say that will relate the verse to the climate of conflict which is its *raison d'être* than Gwendolyn Brooks's introduction to the volume: "He [Lee] knows that the black man today must ride full face into the whirlwind—with small regard for 'correctness,' with limited concern for the possibilities of 'error.' He knows that there are briefs even for the Big Mistake. The Big Mistake is at least a violent Change—and in the center of a violent Change are the seeds of creation."[55]

This view of Lee's poetry is given wider application in a foreword to *New Negro Poets: USA,* in which Miss Brooks says:

> At the present time, poets who happen also to be Negroes are twice-tried. They have to write poetry and they have to remember that they are Negroes. Often they wish that they could solve the Negro question once and for all, and go on from such success to the composition of textured sonnets or buoyant villanelles about the transience of a raindrop, or the gold-stuff of the sun. *They* are likely to find significances in those subjects not instantly obvious to their fairer fellows. The raindrop may seem to them to represent racial tears—and these might seem, indeed, other than transient. The golden sun might remind them that they are burning. In the work of most of today's Negro poets the reader will discover evidence of double dedication, hints that the artists have accepted a two-headed responsibility. . . .
>
> In 1950, I remarked in *Phylon,* "Every Negro has 'something' to say. Simply because he is a Negro, he cannot escape having important things to say. His mere body, for that matter, is an eloquence. His quiet walk down the street is a speech to his people. Is a rebuke, is a plea, is a school. But no real artist is going to be content with offering raw materials." This is as true today—when we, white and black, are a collective pregnancy that is going to proceed to its inevitability, getting worse before it gets better.[56]

Quentin Hill confirms some of Miss Brooks's words when he says:

> Black words do not exist in this country apart from the minds and voices of black people. . . . The purpose of black poetry is

55. Don L. Lee, *Don't Cry, Scream* (Detroit: Broadside Press, 1969), p. 9. Reprinted by permission of the publisher.

56. From Langston Hughes (ed.), *New Negro Poets: USA* (Bloomington: Indiana University Press, 1966), p. 13. Reprinted by permission of the publisher.

> to evoke response in its audience, the black masses, since ideally it is the mass of black people who are speaking. . . . *I hope to wake up one morning in a land where I can write anything I want to, for part of the creative process is choosing what one wants to create rather than creating what one has to.* [My italics.] [57]

I am sure that a synthesis is possible between what one *has* to create and what one *wants* to create: the product is beautiful and powerful art. Gwendolyn Brooks is a clear example of this synthesis. In his less problematic moments, LeRoi Jones is too. This process surely avoids waste. Nothing can become ritual if it is simply an offering of raw material, if it simply tries to photograph or record sensory impressions. I think that most things one *has* to say but does not really want to create can best be said in journalistic or pamphleteering prose. Charles Patterson's poem "Listen" [58] is another remarkably moving piece of synthesis. It penetrates the blood and vibrates in one's system. The poem needs to be reproduced in full:

> Hear the sound
> It is un-like any other
> The ears are in constant pain
> From the sound
> Of Blood dripping from a wound
> Centuries long
> Each drop that falls crashes into time
> Quickly drys and waits for another drop of agony
> Descending like war bombs
> Composed of destruction
> Listen with one ear for the sound
> Cover both—you are there
> Living the sound

57. From Clarence Major (ed.), *The New Black Poetry* (New York: International Publishers, 1969), pp. 139–140. Reprinted by permission of International Publishers Co., Inc.

58. From Clarence Major (ed.), *The New Black Poetry* (New York: International Publishers, 1969), p. 98. Reprinted by permission of International Publishers Co., Inc.

Hear the Blood ooze from the wound
Falling through time
On ears which are deaf to transition
Stop listen to the sound
It is un-like any other
Touch it squeeze it between space
Now attempt to wash it off
Fingers which are bleeding into time
Cup the sound, imprison it.
Then open time's doors and let loose
Your misery and awaken deaf mute men

The futility of bohemianism that wallows in the grease of its own indolence and apathy cannot escape us when the late Ray Durem says:

Man, there were no hypes at Stalingrad,
and Malcolm X is real!
Spare us the cavils of the nihilistic beats
who criticize the cavities and contours of their nest,
but never leave it.
Warm in its filth,
maggots in a rotten apple,
with their little pen or paintbrush
They deride the filth they feed on,
they flutter but they never fly.
. . . .
Man, like,
when you tire of pot
try thought.[59]

Helen Quigless's "Concert" is a lyrical statement that says black is beautiful in a beautiful and memorable idiom:

59. From Ray Durem, "The Inverted Square (A Problem in Social Geometry)" in Ray Durem, *Take No Prisoners* (London: Paul Breman Limited, 1971). Copyright Dorothy Durem 1971. Reprinted by permission of the publisher.

That princely black
dreams aloud the
agony of his race

as his lips grip
the telescopic view
which curves abruptly
and stares upon their face

Sailing through the air,
a taloned-shriek
draws blood from the ears.[60]

And the cry from the music rings against museum stone walls, the city, the dying sun's light, the lilies, the gold fish. It disturbs minds that hate, that tolerate white savagery.

Rings cry the long until
it shudders and dies,
and sweetness comes to him.[61]

There is a considerable volume of the new poetry in Clarence Major's anthology *The New Black Poetry* and Langston Hughes's collection *New Negro Poets: USA* that, together with the verse in the single-author volumes, does not obviously evoke black pride. Yet this evocation is built in and is carried by the tone of the poetry. The prose sense of the poetry tells us what it feels like to be a black American. We see in these two anthologies, as in the single volumes of poetry by LeRoi Jones, Don L. Lee, Larry Neal, Dudley Randall, and others, a revitalizing of language. It ushers in a second "Negro Renaissance" in this century. And yet if we look at the poetics that I began picking my way through, we realize this is what poetry should have been doing since man gave that first cry to articulate his feelings. Something happened to poetry subsequently that turned it into

60. From Clarence Major (ed.), *The New Black Poetry* (New York: International Publishers, 1969), p. 102. Reprinted by permission of International Publishers Co., Inc.
61. *Ibid.*, pp. 47–48.

a mere cerebral activity for the poet's own private amusement or that of his coterie. This was one of the aberrations of alienated Western man. It was thus, all over again, conflict and challenge that were to shake up poetry into an awareness of a mission.

Poem Counterpoem, by Margaret Danner and Dudley Randall, contains the searing "Ballad of Birmingham" by Randall.[62] The child asks her mother to allow her to go to the Freedom March in the streets of Birmingham. No, she may not go, because the dogs are fierce and wild; the clubs and hoses and guns will be at the ready. After pleading again unsuccessfully, the child must go to church. "The mother smiled to know her child/Was in the sacred place." And she smiles the last smile. That explosion in the church wiped it off.

Margaret Danner's "This Is an African Worm" draws an eloquent ironical picture of the Negro:

> This is an African worm
> but then a worm in any land
> is still a worm.[63]

It will not run, stand up before the butterflies who used to be worms too. But then that's all a worm can do—"crawl and wait."

A thundering tribute is paid to Malcolm X by Sonia Sanchez in her *Homecoming* volume. She has no use for martyrdom,

> though I too shall die
> and violets like castanets
> will echo me.[64]

Malcolm will never speak again. But each winter

> I'll breathe
> his breath and mourn

62. Margaret Danner and Dudley Randall, *Poem Counterpoem* (Detroit: Broadside Press, 1966), p. 4. Reprinted by permission of the publisher.

63. *Ibid.*, p. 11.

64. Sonia Sanchez, *Homecoming* (Detroit: Broadside Press, 1969), p. 15. Reprinted by permission of the publisher.

my gun-filled nights.
He was the sun that tagged
the western sky and
melted tiger-scholars
while they searched for stripes

Although she doesn't believe in dying, she feels death in her pulse:

What might have been
is not for him/or me
but what could have been
floods the womb until i drown

"Look for me in the whirlwind/with you," Larry Neal begins his poem "Garvey's Ghost."[65] Garvey has become for some revolutionary black Americans a symbol of upstanding independent blackness. His failure was to them a noble one. The sentiments that impelled him to want to cut loose from white trusteeship, however misdirected, seem basic to the black man's innermost desire today. Neal imagines he hears Garvey's ghost speak from behind

fire smeared faces
and burning black voices; the best
that we would be
in the whirlwind's pain.

He can be found in the "thunder rhythm,"

in the whirlwind's thunder
with the weak one's crawling,
reaching to become that which we would be.

But who has stolen the Negro's voice and eyesight? Will the whirlwind be his doom? The whirlwind knows no color; it "knows only truth and vengeance."

Garvey, who was originally West Indian, seems to think that

65. Larry Neal, *Black Boogaloo* (San Francisco: Journal of Black Poetry Press, 1969), p. 20. Reprinted by permission of the author.

Jamaica was relatively serene, which the black American could not have known. Neal expresses this in the elegiac tone in which words fall soft on the reader's mind, without a loud and crude bounce as it were:

> Jamaica rhythms are soft to feel
> when you understand that quiet
> moments are what a man also needs
> below the surface of things;
> . . . .
> but these things you have never
> really known or seen; a sea of your
> own, your own green hope, your own
> thing, your own sunlight.
> None of these you have known;
> but one continual cry is all,
> one long historical moan
> is all you have known
> one continuous moan in the blues
> kissed whirlwind

Just in case someone wondered if the mood of angry protest one finds in this body of poetry, which swings between the elegiac and apocalyptic tones, is not a self-indulgence, this last stanza should provide an answer. No man in his right senses and with a healthy personality wants perennial conflict. While one's poetry is a way of coping with conflict, it is made an art by these poets, so that it extends into the future.

Your ancestors tried to look beyond the clouds, their gaze searching for a bleeding Christ. Maybe you too, with your contemporaries, thought there might be hope "up" there. You thought you heard somebody knocking at the door, saying, "Sinner, why don't you answer?" You won't answer, of course. Because it is the policeman kicking at the door. The Man has decided to live by the cult of violence. You can't stand on your dignity by forgiving, while the lives of your people are being brutalized. If you don't yourself carry the gun, it is only because you don't have the temperament for it, or else the law and its own guns deter you. To give it a moral justification, which falsely presupposes that the other man *intends* to be guided by a healthy sense of human justice is, in the average man, an act of self-abasement. So your poetry becomes a way of asserting your dignity, with the hope that it will fire your readers with the same sentiments. You'll scream from the very center of your bowels, while the poisonous juices flow liberally into whatever must contain them. You reach saturation point. You do or write something else and when saturation has been relieved, you come back into circulation and you've got to ride the whirlwind. Speech, in your case, poetic speech, as a way of looking for your feelings and attitudes and expressing them, is also an instrument of refinement. The American poet Karl Shapiro wrote a few years ago: "Literature is an accurate transcription of the quality of thought and feeling of the writer and his people. . . . A great literature leaves nothing out—that's its greatness. . . . But to leave nothing out means to go against the grain; it means to dissent." [66]

III

I have explored black American and Caribbean poetry and its relation to conflict. There exists now a Black Arts Movement in America, which is, as Larry Neal says,

> radically opposed to any concept of the artist that alienates him from his community. Black Art is the aesthetic and spiritual sister of the Black Power concept. As such, it envisions an art that speaks directly to the needs and aspirations of Black America. . . . The Black Arts Movement proposes a radical re-ordering of the western cultural aesthetic. It proposes a separate symbolism, mythology, critique, and iconology. . . . It is the opinion of many Black writers, I among them, that the Western aesthetic has run its course: it is impossible to construct anything meaning-

66. Quoted in Sarah Webster Fabio, "A Black Paper," *Negro Digest* (July, 1969), p. 89. Copyright © July 1969 by *Negro Digest*. Reprinted by permission of *Black World* and Sarah Webster Fabio.

> ful within its decaying structure. . . . The cultural values inherent in western history must either be radicalized or destroyed, and we will probably find that even radicalization is impossible. In fact, what is needed is a whole new system of ideas.[67]

Neal quotes Brother Knight on the "black aesthetic":

> To accept the white aesthetic is to accept and validate a society that will not allow him to live. The Black artist must create new forms and new values, sing new songs (or purify old ones); and along with other Black authorities, he must create a new history, new symbols, myths and legends (and purify old ones by fire). And the Black artist, in creating his own aesthetic, must be accountable for it only to the Black people.[68]

Larry Neal continues to say that a "black aesthetic" presupposes the existence of the basis for it. It amounts to an "African-American" cultural tradition. Yet it goes beyond that tradition because it must use some elements of Third World culture (which, incidentally, will also have a tinge of Latin, Asian, and maybe even Oceanic cultures). The ethics linked up with such an aesthetic will ask the question: Whose vision of the world is finally more meaningful—ours or the white oppressors'? What is truth? Whose truth will be valid—that of the oppressor or oppressed?

> In a context of world upheaval, ethics and aesthetics must interact positively and be consistent with the demands for a spiritual world. Consequently, the Black Arts Movement is an ethical movement. Ethical, that is, from the viewpoint of the oppressed.[69]

Poetry, says the black aesthetic, is a "concrete function, an action," not abstractions. Poems are "physical entities: fists, daggers, airplane poems, and poems that shoot guns." LeRoi Jones's poem "Black Art" makes this quite clear:

67. Larry Neal, "The Black Arts Movement." First published in *The Drama Review,* Volume 12, Number 4 (T40), Summer 1968, p. 29. © 1968 by *The Drama Review*. Reprinted by permission. All rights reserved.

68. *Ibid.,* p. 30.

69. *Ibid.,* p. 30.

> Poems are bullshit unless they are
> teeth or trees or lemons piled
> on a step. Or black ladies dying
> of men leaving nickel hearts
> beating them down. Fuck poems
> and they are useful, would they shoot
> come at you, love what you are,
> breathe like wrestlers, or shudder
> strangely after peeing. We want live
> words of the hip world, live flesh &
> coursing blood. Hearts and Brains
> Souls splintering fire. We want poems
> like fists beating niggers out of Jocks
> or dagger poems in the slimy bellies
> of the owner-jews . . .[70]

"Poems are transformed from physical objects into personal forces":

> . . . Put it on him poem. Strip him naked
> to the world. Another bad poem cracking
> steel knuckles in a jewlady's mouth
> Poem scream poison gas on breasts in green berets . . .

This whole idea, of course, that poetry comes to express the collective conscious and unconscious of a community is basically what Caudwell says. When the black aesthetic comes to demonstrate itself in poetry, we are most likely to find that we have merely returned poetry to its original purpose; that we are simply talking about the black experience in a communicable language, and that in the process we are pushing Black Power. What will be new, and is already observable as new, is the release of language brought about by the experience, the content of the poetry. Its audience will be the very public whose consciousness it represents, and for whom the ritual is meant. That tension between the private experience and its expression in public terms will continue, but it will also represent

70. *Ibid.*, p. 31.

that real-life tension between the individuality of a person and social demands. The social demands will be another new feature: they will have reference to black people. The aesthetic and the critical standards it fashions emerge as a community realizes itself, its aspirations, which in turn go to define its cultural destiny. Without these processes, critical standards will shoot out like a New Year's Eve rocket, explode into myriad sparks and fizzle out.

Black poetry, as I see it, is trying to arrange a harmonizing of goals among black people, which are at present so diverse, so disoriented. This is precisely what it is all about. One can speculate on whether white dissent may not eventually merge with Negro dissent whether the blacks like it or not, even if they withdraw at this stage; on what the inevitability will be, which Gwendolyn Brooks senses the black and white "collective pregnancy" will move toward, with things getting worse before they get better. Also, is it not possible that the original springs of poetry, its purpose, its restatement of a communal consciousness, will one day inform white poetry and yank *that* into line with the black man's purpose?

Where a civilization has powerful instruments which maintain its power structure, it can either swallow up a minority culture that challenges it or is passive. Or it can sponsor such a minority culture, promote it, and thereby blunt the edge of its revolt or render the revolt pointless. And then the two can accommodate each other. *Négritude* was placated in this way. In America, there are signs that whites want to sponsor Black Power so as to be able to live with it. They may just decide to sponsor it at the revolutionary level so as to appear genuine and generous friends. What then? LeRoi Jones says he would take the money but knows they won't give it: at any rate unless *they* can decide where and how it is to be used.

Every so often in his critical writings T. S. Eliot says things that make plenty of sense to me. He says, for instance, that the poet "keeps the language from deteriorating or getting ossified." But it is language as a social force, not words for words' sake. A people and its language can deteriorate or advance together.

"It is the capacity of a people to produce the writer as artist that prevents a people from sinking to a condition where a short scale of farmyard noises will provide all the vehicle it needs for expression and communication."[71] Eliot discounts the opinion that only the value of ideas gives a poem its value or that ideas or beliefs do not matter. He also rejects the idea that any one social class or educated minority must make the poet's following. Of course after having rejected this or that, Eliot remains uncertain about the function of poetry. But he has taken us back to what poetry should never have departed from, at any rate in theory.

Reflecting further upon the idea of a black aesthetic, I find myself asking what elements of the Western system of aesthetics the leaders of the Black Arts Movement might be thinking of abandoning, which, if any, he might want to retain. Would he want to reject, for instance:

1. Western form and structure?
2. The use of the "objective correlative," i.e., the use of "a set of objects, a situation, a chain of events" which arouse a particular emotion—in other words, the objectifying of emotions through their sensuous concrete equivalents?
3. Western civilization—Christian or otherwise—which informs many a poet's imagery or symbolism and point of view?
4. The exploitation of multiple levels of meaning sparked off from stated meaning?
5. The Western concept that *mere* exhortation or *mere* propaganda does not make "memorable speech" that true poetry is?
6. The Western ideal for the reader to attain complete *imaginative* identification of himself with the experience presented in a work of art?
7. The enriching of the reader's emotional experience out of the poet's metaphorical or symbolic presentation of fact,

71. T. S. Eliot, "The Writer as Artist," *The Listener,* No. 620 (November 28, 1940), p. 773. Reprinted by permission of Faber & Faber.

a presentation that "universalizes" the particular experience—a process that so often cuts across cultural barriers?

There may be other elements of the Western aesthetic, but I consider the above-mentioned crucial to it. Knowing what is being rejected may throw light on what the new product will be—how uniquely black it will be. The kind and quality of experience, point of view, a new kind of symbolism may give art a uniquely black character. But new symbols are always being created in the Western tradition and here one becomes skeptical about a black uniqueness.

The point of view can include ethics when there is an ethic common to the black writer and to the black reader. Point of view can also include the element of ritual I have referred to before: ritual in the sense in which Maulana Ron Karenga, a Black Power leader, says: "Black Art must be for the people, by the people, and from the people. That is to say, it must be functional, collective, and committing." All take part in ritual, but only at the meeting point between the writer's self-expression and the community's interests and aspirations; in other words, only when the community will want to recite the poetry and dramatize their emotions through it.

A distinctively black experience can also be furnished by legend and myth, as well as by the descriptive presentation of day-to-day happenings. These are all elements one can see constituting a uniquely black art. Is emotion culturally based? Perhaps in the manner of acting it out, yes. But then to try to use this idea as something that distinguishes black art is not saying anything new. Black music, black dance movements are culturally distinctive.

Nor does it help us to say Western man sees form as more important than content or the moral purpose of art. It has not always been like this in the Western tradition. A great work of art in this tradition makes the distinction between form and content irrelevant: they are interlocked, defining and shaping each other. In terms of standard form, fiction offers nothing tangible one can reject: a novel can be anything that tells a story, anyone can colonize it. Clearly, we have still to arrive at the standards of the aesthetic we are talking about. Those who are in the lead, like Larry Neal, LeRoi Jones, Ed Bullins (editor of *Black Theatre Magazine*), Robert Macbeth (director in the New Lafayette Theatre), are honest enough to indicate that they are still probing and groping. Robert Macbeth says in an interview with the poet Marvin X:

> It's still a white western form. . . . The element of a formal play, that is, a story to be told by people acting it out on stage—not acting it out but in conversation on the stage. That's really only partially what it is. I might not be able to describe to you. . . . I know as a director that there are white western elements that I can't help. . . . The ritual form will be, of course, the form that we will follow, the form the western world calls audience-participation, but there is no audience as far as I'm concerned . . . no actors . . . the separation is very slim.[72]

It seems that theater, by the very nature of the medium as an audio-visual art, will arrive at a distinctively black aesthetic sooner. The representation of experience in visual and dramatic terms can, better than either poetry or fiction, realize its own grammar inch by inch as the movement of the drama engages the integrated sensibilities of the chief characters and the rest of the house, until the phrase "audience participation" becomes irrelevant.

In *The Crisis of the Negro Intellectual,* Harold Cruse writes off the Harlem Renaissance of the 1920's because its "ability to foment revolutionary ideas about culture and society (was) smothered"; because it failed to wed its ideas to institutional forms. One such institutional form is theater. The movement did not encourage an ethnic theater because there failed to emerge a body of Negro playwrights. I do not think that as an upsurge of literary expression, albeit in diverse keys of voice, the Harlem Renaissance can honestly be dismissed. For all its aimlessness in sociocultural terms, it represented a new Negro

72. "The Black Ritual Theatre," an interview by Marvin X with Robert Macbeth in *Black Theatre,* No. 3 (1969), pp. 19–24. Reprinted by permission of *Black Theatre.*

consciousness, an important landmark in the tradition of Negro letters. The period of the Dunbars was dead and gone. This the Renaissance made quite clear.

Of course Harold Cruse is dead right in his comment regarding an ethnic theater as a distinctive imprint in the cultural life of a group. Apart from subject matter, there is little if anything that distinguishes the English and French poetry and fiction of Africa as *African*. But the new theater of Africa owes its indigenous character to form and structure as well. Its audience is also miscellaneous, cutting across the lines that normally separate the enlightened from the illiterate. Accordingly, if any form of literary expression among the American Negroes is going to evolve an ethnic aesthetic, it will have to be drama; an aesthetic such as we find in blues, jazz, soul music, the rhythms of dance, and independent Negro religious worship.

And yet it cannot be said that the Harlem school of the 1920's resisted nationalism entirely. Indeed the Harlem Renaissance was full of contradictions. Charles S. Johnson, an editor of the new school, said: "The new racial poetry of the Negro is the expression of something more than experimentation in a new technique. It marks the birth of a new racial consciousness and self-conception. . . . It lacks apology, the wearying appeals to pity, and the conscious philosophy of defense." [73]

Langston Hughes wrote at the time: "We younger Negro artists who create now intend to express our individual dark-skinned selves without fear or shame. If white people are pleased we are glad. If they are not, it does not matter. . . . If colored people are pleased we are glad. If they are not, their displeasure doesn't matter either. We build our temples for tomorrow." [74]

So, while one person was asserting the Negro's ethnic nationalism, another was ambivalent about his audience. The white reviewer and critic stood at the door to the hall of fame, and the readership of the time was mostly white. It did in fact matter

73. From Abraham Chapman (ed.), *Black Voices* (New York: New American Library, 1968), p. 527.

74. *Ibid.*, p. 527.

if the Negro audience was displeased. Hughes later caught on to this. Otherwise he would not have traveled the length and breadth of this nation reading his poetry in a way only the poets of the 1960's have begun to do.

While Negro business was focusing its energies on the black consumer, the writer had to sell his material to the more economically powerful segment of America—the whites. While the Harlem School was striving to correct the image of the Negro that the Dunbars and the assimilationist novelists of the nineteenth century had created, as a reaction against white anti-abolitionism, it was accommodating and riding on the back of white patronage, often of a dubious pedigree. And while this was going on, Alain Locke, that remarkable source of inspiration for the Harlem Renaissance and its major commentator, was affirming: "The Negro mind has leapt . . . upon the parapets of prejudice and extended its cramped horizons. In so doing it has linked up with the growing group consciousness of the dark-peoples and is gradually learning their common interests." He was also reaffirming the Negro's ethnic identity in the areas of blues, spirituals, thought and speech idioms—"the vein that emphasizes the growing historical sense of a separate cultural tradition." [75]

At the same time, in its modern idiom, Negro poetry was, like white American poetry, experimenting with new techniques. The "new" poetry that had begun in 1912 attained its highest quality during World War I before Jean Toomer could leap on to the scene with an imagistic idiom that bristles and quivers with a new life, such as we find in *Cane* (1922). Countee Cullen followed in a similar vein if with less terseness in *Color* (1925). Langston Hughes was to exploit the idiom to the fullest, beginning with *The Weary Blues* a year later. The style these poets used came from the Imagists via Harriet Monroe, Amy Lowell, Pound, Marianne Moore, Vachel Lindsay, Hilda Doolittle. This was a happier contradiction about the Harlem School than the others I have mentioned. The language that

75. *Ibid.*, p. 522.

was most naturally available to the Negro poets had to be that which the whites were trying to evolve to assert a native American sensibility. Claude McKay, on the other hand, expressed a new feeling in a formal manner that mitigated much against the impact such new feeling would be expected to generate. His "Harlem Dancer" (1917), Arna Bontemps says, represents a "poetry written from experience differing from poetry written from books and other cultural media." Together with other anthologizers, Bontemps regards the poem as marking the beginning of the new Harlem mood. Yet it is conventional, loaded with epithets which the poet overworks to do the feeling for him. This defeats the twentieth-century mood. In a strange way, it seems this stilted use of idiom says much about McKay's criticism of what he considered as the aimlessness of the Harlem movement; about his own conflict between the radical white left wing with which he was associated and Garveyist nationalism; about his sense of universality; about his eventual withdrawal from the Harlem scene.

Once the Negro muse had been unchained, the writers of the Harlem Renaissance simply gloried in the ability to express themselves and the freedom to do so. They were for the most part "makers" and not critics. They were out to celebrate. To produce an ethnic theater in the face of a dominant aggressive culture that operates like a vacuum cleaner, a community needs a tough-minded ideology. Not a fugitive ideology like Garvey's, but one that can exploit native roots 300 years deep. We come back to the question of economics, don't we?—the economics of ghetto life, the economics of theater, etc. The Harlem School just had no control over intellectual pursuits that can only be realized through economic power, whatever else Alain Locke's perceptiveness led him to hope for. And the whole thing that bedeviled their intellectual pursuits is even more acute in the 1970's than it was then because of a newer and sharper awareness of it: the relationship between the sense of ethnic belonging and self-assertion on the one hand and the sense of Americanism on the other.

Critic and scholar Saunders Redding expresses in excruciating terms this dilemma, which he calls "cultural dualism." In the act of asserting his rights as an American, the Negro ruthlessly severed himself from his African cultural roots. Of the Harlem School he writes:

> Cultural nationalism raised its head and demanded that literature be patriotic, optimistic, positive, uncritical. . . . Fortunately there was more than faith and fat imagination in some of these works. There was also talent. Had this not been so, Negro writing would have come to nothing for perhaps another quarter of a century, for the ground would not have been plowed for the seeds of later talents. But Du Bois, Johnson, McKay, Fisher, Cullen, Hughes knew what they were about.[76]

Back to our inquiry into contemporary poetry. We seem to be all agreed that, as Addison Gayle, Jr., says in the introduction to his anthology *Black Expression,* there are "experiences universal in character, which form the basis of competent literature"—experiences which Negroes naturally share.[77] We are agreed that all meaningful art has moral implications. We should be free enough to say this without necessarily asking the writer to preach to or at us. The writer can, especially if he is writing fiction, which requires the dramatic method, suggest the moral implications through metaphor or symbolism. This is what Ralph Ellison means when he says, "for me . . . the narrative is the meaning," acknowledging for the reader the right and intelligence to perceive and make his moral judgments. As it happens, *Invisible Man does* give a guide toward a moral judgment, no matter how one interprets it. Of course someone else may say that the reader must be told *how* to interpret it. But this must assume that the writer is inherently a righteous person—a responsibility too terrifying to contemplate.

Addison Gayle says: "the Negro critic approaches the work of art from a moral perspective. . . . This is not to imply that

76. *Ibid.,* p. 616.

77. From *Black Expression* by Addison Gayle, Jr. Pages ix–xv. Copyright © 1969 Weybright and Talley, Inc. Reprinted by permission of the publisher.

the Negro critic eschews aesthetics. . . . Aesthetics are a necessary requirement of art." On this we are all agreed. We are also agreed that the Negro critic has rightly "demanded that the writer concentrate on life, that life, despairing, laughing, hoping, and dying, in the ghettos of this country." But it is not necessary to imply by this that it is a kind of criticism that is alien to the Western tradition. If it is, then there are very many rebels, like the poet Karl Shapiro, critic Caudwell, and all those critics from Aristotle to Tolstoy who have demanded that literature should have a moral value. It seems to be merely a question of emphasis.

The point I want to make is that Western critical standards have been challenged time and again by writers and critics of the West (and this includes European Russia). True enough, the statements that Ralph Ellison, Stanley Braithwaite, and James Baldwin made, cited by Addison Gayle, Jr., are fragments of the Western critical code. Ellison asked that his fiction "be judged as art; if it fails, it fails aesthetically." Braithwaite said: "the highest allegiance (of Negro poetic expression) is to poetry," even though it "hovers for the moment pardonably perhaps, over the race question." Baldwin felt that the only concern of the artist was "to recreate out of the disorder of life that order which is art." But they are only *fragments* of Western aesthetics. Taken singly, none of them by itself can answer all the questions we want to ask about art. Not even if all three were taken together. They need to be consolidated with several other principles to measure up to the great diversity of artistic expression we see today. Of course, I would first have to understand quite clearly whether Braithwaite and I expect the same things of what he calls "poetry." I equate poetry, for instance, with the inner meaning or truth of anything in space and time. If he means the same thing, I could apply his statement to a considerable body of good black verse. So could I apply Baldwin's general statement, short of accepting the statement that it is the *only* concern of the artist. If Ellison means by "aesthetically" only form, stylistics, and everything else but content, then I cannot apply his criterion to a work like Amos

Tutuola's or any other novel that sprawls almost shapelessly in similar fashion and yet is still good, meaningful fiction.

I am not making apologies for the perversion of certain regions of Western aesthetics and their resultant failure to assert the moral purpose of art. I am socialist and humanist and cannot condone, for instance, the stupidities and perversions of art that often result from the ethic of free enterprise and the greed that goes with it. Nor can I take seriously the people who urge that the true spiritual asylum for the black man is Islam and try to construct an aesthetic around the essence of their newfound fetish which they bluff themselves into thinking is higher, worthier, more liberating than the Christian fetish. I cannot support the common assertion among some Western critics who claim that bitterness must always produce bad art. I can't stand the obtuseness of men like Louis Simpson, whom Hoyt Fuller quotes as saying of Gwendolyn Brooks's *Selected Poems*: "I am not sure it is possible for a Negro to write well without making us aware he is a Negro. On the other hand, if being a Negro is the only subject, the writing is not important." [78] I am infuriated by neurotics like David Littlejohn, who reads an attack on whites into every line of black fiction: "Surely the insult, the anti-white affront is not entirely an accident of the creative unconscious." [79] He may be right in reading the symbols this way, but he has decided to open only this channel of his response mechanism. He is determined right from the outset, as his Introduction indicates, to treat Negro writing as "the product of small minds that happen to be Negro." Often one wonders whether it is the prison the black man is trying to break out of in real life that Mr. Littlejohn is indignant about, or the mere fact that the prison is symbolically suggested.

What I am trying to warn against is the danger of finding ourselves having, out of sheer crusading zeal, dismissed elements

78. From "Toward a Black Aesthetic," by Hoyt Fuller. Reprinted from *The Critic*. Copyright © 1968 by the Thomas More Association, 180 N. Wabash Ave., Chicago, Ill. 60601.

79. From *Black on White: A Critical Survey of Writing by American Negroes*. Copyright © 1966 by David Littlejohn, Grossman Publishers, N.Y. Page 5.

of Western aesthetics which are either built into our new modes of expression or which have been or are already being challenged by Western critics. In the event, we cannot then imagine that we are doing anything uniquely black. We may just have been doing the same thing separately, for ourselves. Clearly, what is referred to as a black aesthetic has emerged as a *black point of view* so far.

It is an axiom to say that only the black man can write authentically about being black. But it is most doubtful that, as some people suggest, the only reader who can understand, enter into the emotion of such a work of art, and share it, must be black; or put in another way, that a white reader can never do this. Richard Gilman has said as much of Eldridge Cleaver's *Soul on Ice*. He said that Cleaver's book and Malcolm X's autobiography were "unassimilable for those of us who aren't black. . . . Negro suffering is not of the same kind as ours." Cleaver's writing "remains in some profound sense not subject to correction or emendation or, most centrally, approval or rejection by those of us who are not black." [80] Indeed, his conclusion was that he and his fellow whites should suspend judgment on Negro writing.

This is too easy a way out of the difficulty of being taken seriously by those outside one's own ethnic group. It may even be an unwitting refusal on the part of the white man to expose himself completely to the emotional, sensory, and intellectual impact of Cleaver's and Malcolm X's writings, auguring at the same time a permanent blackout for whites in general in relation to black writing.

In this connection, I find Professor Krishna Rayan's article most illuminating.[81] Professor Rayan, formerly of the National

80. Richard Gilman, "White Standards and Negro Writing," from *The Confusion of Realms*, by Richard Gilman (New York: Random House, 1970). (Published originally in *The New Republic*, March 9, 1968, pp. 25–30.) Copyright © 1968 by Richard Gilman. Reprinted by permission of Random House, Inc.

81. Krishna Rayan, "*Rasa* and the Objective Correlative," *The British Journal of Aesthetics*, V, No. 3 (July, 1965), pp. 246–260. Reprinted by permission of *The British Journal of Aesthetics* and Krishna Rayan.

Defense Academy in Poona, India, and at one time visiting Professor at the University of Zambia, is an authority on aesthetics and English-language teaching. According to him, the theory of *Rasa-dhvani*—the suggestion of emotion in art—first made its appearance in Sanskrit literary criticism of the ninth century through the writings of Anandarvardhana. Although T. S. Eliot did not become acquainted with Sanskrit criticism until as recently as 1955, his "objective correlative"—the formulation "that in art, states of sentience are suggested through their sensuous equivalents"—corresponds very closely to the Sanskrit theory.

The central concept of Indian aesthetics, Professor Rayan says, is *rasa,* which literally means tincture, taste, flavor, relish. *Rasa* is "emotion objectified, universalized, . . . growing out of and being a transfiguration of the emotion presented in art." It has "all the features of aesthetic experience familiar to Western philosophy."

In the tenth or eleventh century, Abhinavagupta listed nine permanent emotions, each of which is, when a work of art is being composed and subsequently contemplated by someone else, then elevated to *rasa.* The sexual emotion will, for instance, be elevated to love, amusement to the comic, grief or distress to pathos, anger to another level of itself, masterfulness or energy to the heroic, fear to another level of itself, disgust to another level of itself, wonder to another level of itself, subsidence or quietude to serenity.

All men are potentially capable of realizing *rasa,* provided one is sensitive. The permanent emotions are "together exhaustive, so that whichever emotion the poem or play expresses or arouses, whichever emotion arises in the poet or the character or the actor or the spectator or reader, comes under one (permanent emotion) or the other." Sanskrit theory asserts that a poem presents or conveys an emotion through the objective correlatives of the emotion. "Images, characters, situations which are the objective correlatives of the emotion are presented descriptively in a poem, and when the reader's mind makes contact with these, they awaken the corresponding *sthāyin* (permanent emotion) within him and raise it to the state of *rasa*."

In the Charles Patterson poem "Listen," reproduced earlier, there are objective correlatives like sound; pain; blood from a wound, fresh or dry; bombs; deaf ears; fingers cupping the sound; deaf-mute men. They evoke grief mixed with terror and anger. These emotions are intense, heightened, and richer than the initial raw emotions of anger and grief.

Abhinavagupta, Professor Rayan says, explained that emotion was already there within the reader—as the *sthāyin*. Thus the correlates do not produce or generate it but "render it manifest —as a lighted lamp reveals an existing jar in the room. Emotion emerges from its descriptively presented correlates exactly as the suggested meaning emerges from the word or its meaning—by the operation of the function of suggestion which is inherent in language. Art suggests emotion. Emotion is suggested meaning." Thus, if I say that the poem "Listen" discussed above arouses grief and terror and anger, I am attaching a meaning to the poem that is an emotional response. This is as it should be. The stated meaning comprising the described objects or correlates does not of itself make poetry. Through the heightened emotion, or *rasa,* they arouse, the reader is able to penetrate the unspoken and therefore the essence of the poem.

All emotion in poetry is suggested. Emotion is "the image's resonances." Sanskrit's most valuable contribution to poetics consists in the explanation of how this is done. "Objective-emotion associations for members of the same culture are of course bound to have a high common factor." Now when a man writes a poem to express an emotion, it is not the raw emotion one experiences as when, in real life, one reacts to an immediate stimulus, like anger triggered off by a policeman's savagery manifested physically. The poem is rather a contemplation of or reflection upon the actual emotional experience. The experience has become a piece of knowledge by then. The poem is suggesting the emotion via its objective associates or correlatives. The poet is thus expressing himself in public terms, by presenting objects the knowledge and awareness of which is public. The writing of a poem or fiction or a play is, at a level relevant to us, an act of objectifying one's subjective experience and making it publicly available. If I tell you, "I'm angry," I am not expressing anything like what I really feel, if I am sincere. The best way to approximate the actual thing that is going on inside me is to objectify the emotion, represent it through imagery, suggestive language sparked off by objects, characters, or actors, and so on. (Quite obviously the subconscious comes into play in an artistic representation: a number of things can be suggested which were not in the forefront of the writer's consciousness at the time of composing his piece. We cannot dismiss this dimension in responding to the work.)

If we respond to emotion or suggested meaning in art, which must of necessity have come quite some way up to the high level of the *rasa* since the time it came out in the raw—if this is what happens, how then can a man fail to enter into such an emotion or suggested meaning simply because he comes from outside the poet's racial group? How can he fail, unless he were obtuse, or his racial prejudice or attitude of self-abasement stood in the way and prevented him from *reading* the poem?

"According to the Sanskrit theory about *rasa*," Professor Rayan states with his usual persuasiveness and keen perception, "the emotion which the reader experiences is the same as the emotion presented in the poem—in a heightened version but essentially the same emotion. When Othello suffers, I, the reader, do not pity him—because I am suffering with him. When Beowulf wrestles with Grendel, I do not admire him—because I am with or within him sharing his sense of high enterprise. If I experience fear, it is immediately before and after the murder of Duncan or during the banquet, and not at the end of the play."

This has a lot to teach us. Proponents of a black aesthetic will need to reconcile some basic assertions. If, as Dudley Randall says of the Negro poets, "writing for a black audience out of black experience," that "they are indifferent as to whether their work survives, just so it is effective today,"[82] there must surely be others who at the same time want their work to outlive the present: those who, as Addison Gayle says, are dedicated to "the proposition that literature is a moral force and an aesthetic creation." Another basic assertion is white critic Robert Bone's: "By virtue of his deeper insight, he, the Negro writer can exorcise the demons that threaten his people from within," coupled with Addison Gayle's: "But it is equally true that he can exorcise those demons which, today, rend the American society. For the Negro writer is America's conscience and the Negro critic must be the conscience of them both."[83] Both of which assertions imply a situation that will, although some people will not like to think it, last a good long time. This, together with the very concept of a black aesthetic, cannot imply a short view.

A fourth assertion is Herbert Hill's—that the New Negroes of the 1960's, in relation to their predecessors in the 1930's, "made the creative act their first consideration. . . . As the Negro writer moves beyond anger, he develops a new concern for the writer's craft, for literary discipline and control and seeks an involvement in the larger world of art and ideology."[84]

I am exploring the meaning of poetry in relation to conflict. Poetry has probably reached as high a revolutionary pitch as it could ever attain in the United States. Having dismissed African *négritude*'s claims in this direction, I want to look at the poetry of Senegal's David Diop, South Africa's Dennis Brutus, and Nigeria's Wole Soyinka.

David Diop's poetry has a sharp edge and robustness no other French poetry in West Africa has. It is in the tradition of the angry Caribbean poetry of the late 1920's and 1930's. The colo-

82. From Addison Gayle, Jr. (ed.), *Black Expression* (New York: Weybright & Talley, 1969), p. 112.

83. From *Black Expression* by Addison Gayle, Jr. Page xii. Copyright © 1969 Weybright and Talley, Inc. Reprinted by permission of the publisher.

84. From *Soon, One Morning: New Writing by American Negroes, 1940–1962,* edited by Herbert Hill. Page 4. Copyright © 1963 by Alfred A. Knopf, Inc. Reprinted by permission of the publisher.

nial whites to him are vultures with blood dripping from their talons: the blood is a remembrance of colonial tutelage.

In those days
There was painful laughter on the metallic
hell of the roads
And the monotonous rhythm of the paternoster
Drowned the howling on the plantations
O the bitter memories of extorted kisses
Of promises broken at the point of a gun.[85]
. . . .

In "La Route véritable," the poet warns against the kind of thing the whites flaunt as truth. Black brothers whose youth they have wanted to revile should not seek truth in their affected phrases, in their paternalistic applause and domestic treacheries, in that mask that moves like the real face but "covers with perfume the hideousness of their sores."

. . . .
Truth, beauty love
are the laborer shattering the vicious quiet of their parlors
The woman who grants voluptuous and solemn
The kiss that leaps beyond the limits of reckoning
and the flowers of lovers and the child in loving arms
that is all they have lost, brothers
and which together we shall expose along the world's
thoroughfares.[86]

Diop comes back home from studies abroad, during which he lost his name. He is rediscovering Africa, his name, his people:

85. Translation by George Moore and Ulli Beier. From *Modern Poetry from Africa,* ed. George Moore and Ulli Beier. Copyright George Moore and Ulli Beier, 1963, p. 59. Reprinted by permission of Penguin Books Ltd.

86. David Diop, *Coups de Pilon* (Paris: Présence Africaine, 1961), p. 15. This and the following translations by E. Mphahlele. Reprinted by permission of the publisher.

. . . .
Ten years my love
And the mornings of illusions and the debris of ideas
And nights suffused with alcohol
Ten years and the world has breathed its agony on me.
The pain that loads today with tomorrow's taste
And makes of love a boundless river.[87]
. . . .

He is now back, however, his days will be adorned in "necklaces of laughter," "renewed joys."

The poet mourns the death of Emmett Till in his poem "A Un Enfant noir"—the fourteen-year-old youngster who was lynched in Mississippi in 1955. The only crime the boy committed was to dare to look at a white girl,

A body black boy that only whites can
ravish at orgies to the rhythm of your blues.[88]
. . . .

And the whites saw their social order tottering.

In "L'Agonies de chaînes," Diop sees hyenas beat around the cemetery, the earth soaked with blood; he hears hate rumble down the road:

. . . .
I think of the Vietnamese lying in the ricefields
of the Congolese galley slave,
    brother of the lynched in Atlanta
I think of the macabre trudging of silence
When the wing of steel passes above
    the laughter scarcely born.[89]
. . . .

87. *Ibid.*, p. 26.
88. *Ibid.*, p. 28.
89. *Ibid.*, p. 17.

Their chains strangled hope; the light went out of the lives of those who sweat:

> . . . .
> However, it is the sun that bursts out from our voices
> And from savannah to jungle
> Our hands shrivel in the grip of battle
> Show to those who cry the cries of the future
> . . . .

And the song of the dead carries us to the gardens of life.

Diop died in an air crash in 1960, aged thirty-three. His was the powerful voice of a rebel. Although the poetry is scanty, we can see how very close he was to the center of life that is controlled by whites, how alert he was to the chicanery and corruption in white power.

In colonial Africa where whites did not ever intend to settle, the black man was spared the intensity of physical as well as mental agony that life is for the black South African. Resistance poetry has a relatively virile tradition in South Africa. It has come through to us in the form of such oral epics and praise poems as have survived over the two-and-a-half centuries since the first encounter between white settlers and the blacks whom the former found in the Cape Province. The early poetry that came of the experience of the Wars of Dispossession ending toward the end of the nineteenth century had vitriolic energy. The grandson of Moshoeshoe, king of the then Basutoland, records his triumph as hero of the Gun War of 1880 (between whites and blacks):

> Deep in his pool the crocodile glared,
> He glared with his blood-red eyes,
> And lo! the young White braves were drowned,
> Aye, they fell into the jaws of the snake,
> The black snake, *khanyapa,* King of the Waters.*

* King of the Waters, legendary animal with power to "call" people into the deep pool by merely glaring.

Another of Moshoeshoe's people says:

Arise, ye sons of the Mountain-at-Night!*
the hyena howls, the white hyena,
all ravenous for the bones of Moshoeshoe,
of Moshoeshoe who sleeps high up on the mountain,

its belly hangs heavy and drags on the ground,
all gorged with the bones of warrior-kings;
its mouth is red with the blood of Sandile†

Awake, rock-rabbits of the Mountain-at-Night
she darts out her tongue to the very skies,
that rabbit-snake with female breasts‡
who suckled and fostered the trusting Fingos,
thereafter to eat them alive.

The African Christian, because of his divided loyalty, often became a butt for the sarcasm of others:

. . . they sing in praise of the King
proclaiming Jehovah and Christ:
how strange to us that they turn to him their buttocks,
albeit proclaiming him king! [90]

A poet called Gqoba wrote two "Great Discussions"—one between the "Christian and the Pagan" and the other "On Education." He says if the Christians were truthful, they would admit that in fact they had lost their faith. Their youth were drunkards. The white man who brought Christianity oppresses both pagan and Christian. But the life of the pagan is much richer because the Christian, in spite of self-denial and martyrdom, still fears death which may send him to hell. The pagan looks forward to a happy life among the ancestors when he dies. The poet rails against the converted:

* Literal translation of *Thaba Bosigo,* Moshoeshoe's mountain, flat-topped, accessible only to Basotho climber.

† Black king conquered by the British in the Cape Province.

‡ Queen Victoria.

90. A. C. Jordan's translation from Sesotho, *Africa South,* II, No. 1 (October–December, 1957), pp. 97–105.

Deserting your chiefs, you came to the White man;
destroying our rule, you side with the enemy;
but now your faith is lean and shrivelled
even like a chameleon whose mouth is smeared
with nicotine on a sultry summer's day.

Then followed a period corresponding to the American Negro era of a poetry that merely stated that the black man was oppressed. It did not tell us what the black man really thinks and feels under the yoke. Typical of this school was the late B. W. Vilakazi. On the very rare occasions when he was not writing lyrics about a historical hero or calamity, the Victoria Falls, mornings, stars, the wind, Vilakazi had this to say about the gold mines:

The noise you make must vex my soul
And echo in my ears
Like distant bells of booming brass.
They speak to me of splendid homes
Of men made rich because of me,
Made richer through my poverty;
A bloodless used-up ox am I.

And then:

Because the white men are as stone,
Can you, of iron, not be gentler? [91]

The emergence of poets like Dennis Brutus and Mazisi Kunene is a sign of the excruciating pace and quality of the times. Like Kunene, Dennis Brutus is a man of action. Because of his involvement in the politics of sport as a campaigner against South Africa's participation in international games like the Olympics, Brutus was hounded by the police. He tried to skip the country, but was returned to the South African police by the Portuguese in Mozambique. He was shot in the stomach when he tried to escape. After recovery he was indicted in court

91. *Ibid.*

and sentenced to eighteen months' imprisonment, which he served on Robben Island. After his release he was placed under house arrest for twelve of the twenty-four hours of each day. He came to know, through all his sensory equipment the sound of "sirens, knuckles, boots"—the title of his first volume of verse:[92]

> The sounds begin again
> the siren in the night
> the thunder at the door
> the shriek of nerves in pain

Then faces split by pain, the muted wailing—

> Importunate as rain
> the wraiths exhale their woe
> over the sirens knuckles boots
> my sounds begin again

The images grind and flash and sparkle.

A common hate enriches our love and us, he says. It disgusts us when some people try to escape, become too discreet:

> Rich foods knotted to revolting clots
> of guilt and anger in our queasy guts
> remembering the hungry comfortless.

And yet, somehow we survive; tenderness does not wither. Although boots kick the door, "patrols uncoil along the asphalt dark/hissing their menace to our lives," and the police burst in with searchlights, somehow tenderness survives. Not a weak-kneed tenderness that surrenders to oppression, but ordinary human tenderness among ourselves.

Dennis Brutus's latest volume, *Letters to Martha and Other Poems from a South African Prison,* begins with "Longing." Can logic plus "semantic ambiguities," he asks, neutralize "this simple ache's expletive detonation"? A question all these poets

92. Dennis Brutus, *Sirens, Knuckles, Boots* (Ibadan: Mbari Publications, 1962). There are no page numbers in this book. Reprinted by permission of the author.

must be asking; like Don Lee, who feels his metaphors and stanzas will not stop a .38.

> My heart knows now such devastation,
> Yearning, unworded, explodes articulation:
> Sound-swift, in silence, fall the rains of poison.[93]

The prisoner is assailed by a mixture of feelings after the sentence in court: sick relief, apprehension, hints of brutality, exultation at the thought of challenge, self-pity, and the knowledge that there are others who endure. He goes through the motions. The concrete objects in front of him, the thoughts that rush through his mind, sexual assault:

> tendrils sprout from your guts in a
> hundred directions . . .

Left to himself and his own thoughts,

> In the greyness of isolated time
> which shafts down into the echoing mind,
> wraiths appear, and whispers of horrors
> that people the labyrinth of self.[94]

He also knows fear, a deadly enemy:

> How it seeks out the areas of our vulnerability
> and savages us
> until we are so rent and battered . . .[95]

By way of postscripts, Brutus writes a number of stanzas on several subjects, still in reminiscent mood. Blood River Day for the Boers commemorates the Battle of Blood River of 1838, where they clashed with the Africans. The Boers were on their great trek from the south, in search of country where they

93. From *Letters to Martha* by Dennis Brutus (London: Heinemann Educational Books, 1969), p. 1. Reprinted by permission of the publisher.
94. *Ibid.*, pp. 4, 6.
95. *Ibid.*, p. 23.

would be free of British rule. Every year when the whites commemorate this day, it is to think of their survival in that battle and thank their God for it. It is, as always, to rededicate themselves to the maintenance of white supremacy, to spill blood if need be. Blood has become the main symbol of life for them. They exact that from the black: shoot them in public, hang them in the prisons. As Brutus says:

> Each year on this day
> they drum the earth with their boots
> and growl incantations
> to evoke the smell of blood
> for which they hungrily sniff the air.[96]

On thinking about a mob of whites who attacked those who protested against the Sabotage Bill in Johannesburg, Brutus says:

> These are the faceless horrors
> that people my nightmares
> . . . .
> O my people
> what have you done
> and where shall I find comforting
> to smooth awake your mask of fear
> restore your face, your faith, feeling, tears.[97]

Brutus's poetry in this volume ranges over a diversity of moods. On the road he abandons himself to the serenity of the landscape, the moon, the few stars. He feels a tenderness

> As stars harden to spearpoint brilliance
> and focus fierce demands for peace[98]

Laughter should be abolished first, he says—before things are righted. Or it should

96. *Ibid.*, p. 26.
97. *Ibid.*, p. 36.
98. *Ibid.*, p. 40.

find its gusts reverberate
with shattering force through halls of glass
that artifice and lies have made.

It is mute now because of

train wails, babies' sirens' wails:
jackboots batter the sagging gate
the wolfwind barks where the tinplate gapes,
each snarls apocalyptic anger

When the underdog laughs, hoarse and deep, there is a "smoldering flame" at the bottom of it. He laughs erect, without a jim-crow or sycophant smile:

here laugh moulds heart as flame builds sword.

So don't put down laughter—this flame:

the self at its secret hearth
nurses its smoulder, saves its heat
while oppression's power is charred to dust [99]

A mood of hope, but the questionings continue. He does not hate. He does not belch his anger, it does not bubble up to his eyes, nor does hate fill his breath. Only loneliness is eating into him, immobilizing him.

Then the sense of triumph: he believes that by having succeeded in placing blocks before South African white sport so that it cannot affiliate with international sporting bodies, he has lashed them, they bear the scars of this defeat. He thinks he will do more. They know it, and wish they could tear him up: maybe they will, yet. This time anger ferments in him:

but I accept their leashed-in power
and the cloaked malice of their gaze
and wait
and
anger and resolution

99. *Ibid.*, p. 45.

Yeast in me
waiting for the time of achievement.[100]

Then he will flog these thieves again.

The poet realizes that as God will not answer back during the dialogue he (with his people) has been trying to establish, he would rather damn himself if by rebelling he must bring this upon himself. How shall I feel guilty, he says,

—if He damn me,
drive me to damnation
by inflicting the unendurable
force me along the knife-blades till I choose
perdition,[101]

God is the guilty one. When a God has turned devil, the poet is constrained to cry, "Evil be thou my Good!"

The spiritual battle continues. He cries for pity from God—not mercy, because he wants a fellow feeling; perhaps because God himself is in pain. There remains a lot that cannot be known, "So we/must grapple." Is God the hangman, the torturer?

Must we be driven to the edge
racked on the precipice of the world?
. . . .
Can we find hope
in thinking that our pain
refines us of our evil dross,
prepares us for a splendid destiny?[102]

Dennis Brutus's first published poetry, *Sirens, Knuckles, Boots,* which came out in the early 1960's in Ibadan, displays the usual features of a beginner's work: brash, raw anger wielding the long thundering line and harsh sounds.

In *Letters to Martha,* the long thundering line and awkward

100. *Ibid.,* p. 52.
101. *Ibid.,* p. 54.
102. *Ibid.,* p. 57.

phraseology have given way to a subdued diction. And yet so much of the collection lapses into talkative verse which sounds like tired prose: like a guitar string that has lost its tension. One tends to condone this lapse because of the singleness of emotion and mood the *Letters* represent. The impact is cumulative.

The promise one senses in the *Letters* is certainly not anywhere near fulfillment in Brutus's later work. *Poems from Algiers* (published by the African and Afro-American Research Institute, University of Texas at Austin) is disappointing. There is nothing important the poems say, no specific emotion they can be said to be conveying. Only observational fragments. Two closely connected factors must account for this poverty: the poignant condition of exile that does not even have a base around which one's creative energies can regroup and rediscover their language; Brutus's ambivalence about the value of poetry or any other kind of creative writing in the present struggle against South African fascism. He has for ten years and more been at the head of a movement that is campaigning against racism in South African and international sport. So far the focus has been to bring about the expulsion of South Africa from the Olympics and international sports bodies. Brutus travels widely for this purpose and also to organize aid for the defense of political prisoners in southern Africa. He feels the inner compulsion to write poetry, but he does not concede that it is important enough to warrant time off to organize his energies, to collect himself, and to hammer out a language that will match his sincerity of passion. And yet that impulse to communicate through the means of verse will not let him be. He feels guilty about not writing and yet will feel equally guilty for spending that much time writing.

It was desperately necessary to leap out of oppression that sapped one's creative blood, and yet we exiles spend years searching for asylum, physical and spiritual. Involuntary exile implies a rejection of place and a hangup about the place one has rejected and a denial for much of the time of the possibility of a fit substitute. Dennis Brutus says in an unpublished poem:

I *am* the exile
am the wanderer
the troubadour
(whatever they say)

gentle I am, and calm
and with abstracted pace
absorbed in planning,
courteous to servility

but wailings fill the chambers of my heart
and in my head
behind my quiet eyes
I hear the cries and sirens.

You play a single melody that has relevance to a time and indeterminate place, but always the unarticulated backdrop, the South African in you, haunts you. Maybe one can yet create poetry out of the very experience of exposure to and immersion in more cultures than one . . .

Keorapetse Kgositsile is another poet writing in exile. He fled South African fascism in the early 1960's and now lives in the United States. Although he has been settled in one place longer than Brutus has been in England, and he has been continuously in America since he arrived, his poetry shows another aspect of exile—that of the relationship between writer and audience. Kgositsile naturally came under the influence of the black American poets of the 1960's. He even affirmed some of their attitudes toward the "white Negro." As in the poem "For Sons of Sonless Fathers," he says the "white Negro" is

a ghost
more pale than faded junk
lighter than snowflake
not even swayed
by song or dance from there
to here . . .

He is a mere

    ball of transparent pus where
    the manhood used to be
    son of a sonless father.[103]

Why doesn't he wake up to the fact that the "life of those ghouls" he envies is a "death dance without song or natural laughter"? That he is not even his "own possible shadow"?

It is not likely that Kgositsile would adopt this stance if he were talking immediately to a South African audience. This is the diction that is common in the new American Negro poetry that must diminish those blacks who want to be part of the dominant white culture. Although this statement is not inapplicable to South African Negroes, one would not address them in quite the same categorical terms. South African white culture does not permit the black man to assimilate as much of it as it is possible for the Negro here to adopt white American standards, for him to attain economic power within multi-racial trade unions and so on. Envy for the white man's privileges and accompanying value systems there is bound to be in both black worlds. A fighting poetry ignores, involuntarily or by choice, for better or for worse, paradoxes and ironies such envy is often loaded with.

Every so often, when you think Kgositsile has struck on an image which he is going to develop or pursue, he drops it suddenly. You then have the impression of a mind that works in intermittent flashes. One does not know, for instance, why "vampires" is used in the following poem; where "oceans of memory" lead to in their "giantsteps"; whether the childhood that is being "reclaimed" by "the unrelenting tide" emerged from the latter in the first place. We get the message of the poem all right: that although we build slowly, the very act of doing within a definite framework is a way of providing a definite answer:

103. Keorapetse Kgositsile, *My Name Is Afrika* (New York: Doubleday, 1971), p. 86. Copyright © 1971 by Keorapetse Kgositsile. Reprinted by permission of Doubleday & Company, Inc.

Across continents on fire
Vampires fly against the wind
Do we lack specific answer?
Oceans of memory
Giantstep in upright path
The newborn infant asks which
Way is the way to the way
The unrelenting tide sticky
As mountains of wax
Giantsteps
To reclaim the childhood
We rebuild swallow-slow
But we rebuild
How deny specific deed is
Specific answer? SPEAK! [104]

Short sharp statements like the following succeed:

Do not be dis-spirited
Because
You can
Move the wall aside
in
the end
Even when you move to
The outskirts of your honor
Do not be dis-spirited
By the chains of dishonor
Keep on burning
Heaven can wait
Baby this is soultime! [105]

There is here no self-indulgence in mere verbal felicity as we so often find in Kgositsile's verse, particularly his earliest utterances. Also, he achieves relative success when he works from

104. Keorapetse Kgositsile, *For Melba* (Chicago: Third World Press, 1970), p. 12. Reprinted by permission of the publisher.
105. *Ibid.*, p. 14.

or around the "poison finger in the inner regions of the heart," from personal specifics. When he adopts a public stance and he addresses himself to experiences which he may suspect are common to both black worlds, he fails to connect with the particularities of either. And he does not yet have a language that will fulfill his sense of fellow feeling with the American Negro. Always we must keep going back to Kgositsile to locate the center. When he speaks to his mother, to his son, to Africa, to Rap Brown, to Lumumba, and so on, the references are incisive, the voice is clear as a bell. In his "Random Notes to My Son" [106] his muted invective is aimed at those who "speak of black power whose eyes/will not threaten the quick whitening of their own intent," against those who "scream of pride and beauty as though it were not/known that 'Slaves and dead people have no beauty'." He speaks of "confusion and borrowed fears" which suggests the agony of exile, an affirmation of other people's aspirations, borrowed commitment. But if the father has "fallen with all the names" he is,

> The newborn eye, old as
> Childbirth, must touch the day
> That, speaking my language, will
> Say, today we move, we move . . .

Even apart from the peculiar situation of exile and rootlessness, black poets must realize that there is only a general way in which they can express the longings and ideals of black worlds outside their own. Even that event we can only arrive at through our own particular concrete cultural experiences. Although I am African, the Nigerian or the Kenyan or the Zambian experience is alien to me in its cultural specifics. And if I want to explore imaginatively and sympathetically any such experience I cannot afford to skip the specifics. This means I have to be alive to the similarities and parallels and diversities between my experiences and the other black man's at different periods of history. There is another and important level at

106. Kgositsile, *My Name Is Afrika,* p. 26.

which historian John Henrik Clarke says: "It is time for the black writer to draw upon the universal values in his people's experience, just as Sean O'Casey and Sholem Aleichem drew upon the universal values in experiences of the Irish and the Jews."[107]

South African Negro writers wield the language of prose effectively but not of poetry. We lost the heritage of our Bantu poetry which spoke a metaphor and allegory that were native to us. When we were compelled to master English as a lingua franca to meet the demands of black nationalism, when we could have returned to our indigenous languages with dignity (both in oral and written forms), the white rulers had boxed them up and begun to promote literatures in them that glorified white rule and the policy of ethnic divisions. On the other hand, Lesotho, which has always had its own presses, has continued to publish in Sesotho since the nineteenth century. Its indigenous literature has never been subjected to Boer tyranny. It seems reasonable to predict that, as we cannot use our Bantu languages or Afrikaans (which Brutus uses with competence and tremendous force) on existing terms, more and more South African blacks will want to use English as the last post of respectability. And maybe just as our prose writers and jazz musicians learned a lot from American Negro artists, we shall yet find we want to take a leaf from the driving, pressurized verse of the Americans, if only because it represents a release of language and a celebration of survival. Kgositsile has already begun to do this, and one sees in his verse a thrust that cannot but gain power as he matures, and his focus sharpens, and he attains a sense of place.

The black American poets led by LeRoi Jones feel the white man's style of God is too much in the way; He has to be destroyed and replaced by either humanism or the black man's God. Others may have simply suspended belief. Conflict does other things to those who are involved in it, depending on the individual temperament. It is surely this individual tempera-

107. Chapman, *Black Voices,* p. 645.

ment that determines style and distinguishes one poet from another even when poets are driven by a common purpose; even when, as true poetry has done throughout the history of mankind, it represents the sum of the instinctive drives of a community which gives it birth. The black American poets of this half of the twentieth century have, by and large, tacitly and aloud, made a pact to subordinate the individual temperament or will to the creation of a poetry that will be a black expression, a black revolt, a realization of a black consciousness, available to all black men who respond to the battle cry. Not only should the individual personality be subordinated to this major purpose: it must be made to serve the purpose.

In South Africa, as we became disinherited from the integrated drives and myths of our forefathers who had *one* thing to protect (land) and had *one* idea of the enemy and only *one* way to fight him—as we became political fighters, we became poets in a special sense. We wrote, just as the black American writers feel about poets of the first Renaissance, in order to show that we could also write—like whites. Prose fiction then leapt ahead of poetry and is still in the lead in terms of quality, quantity, relevance, and urgency.

That the American Negro is miles ahead of the South African Negro is a measure of the relative abundance of opportunity he has enjoyed, such as his South African counterpart could never have. The white American can be just as savage as the white South African. We all live in ghettos in both countries. But the fact that the *whole* of the black man's life in South Africa is legislated for—from the cradle to the grave; the fact that we have so many political prisoners in South Africa; the fact that education is not free and does not provide for the person who has to leave school to work except in so far as he can follow the white man's instructions in the latter's own language; the fact that although we are culturally self-sufficient, in a way only West African societies are, we do not have the material resources to do half as much as we can and want to do to consolidate our cultural activities and to create a base for more writing to develop; the fact that we do not enjoy the freedom of mobility the black American can boast, whatever the limitations; the fact that at least eight black writers are now living in exile and are banned for the South African readership—all these factors do mean that as writers we are more like disembodied voices that echo from hill to hill. Our audience is as vaguely constituted as that which T. S. Eliot conceived of as "intelligent man." And this won't do. It knocks the bottom out of poetry as ritual. And only as ritual can it contain conflict. The black American can count his blessings. The paradox is that he is in a bag and must exhale and inhale in that bag: he is a minority ethnic group. He can never be in a majority in a so-called democratic form of government. He can only hope to civilize the white man to the degree that the latter can, if he is chosen to, represent his views and aspirations in government. This is a very, very distant and thin hope. He can demand a separate state: most whites would happily finance such a state in order to get the black man off their conscience. No, it just won't do to press for a separate state. Why make it this easy for the white man? Let them live together. Maybe the black man will need to sustain, if he *can* sustain, the present mood of withdrawal, of pulling out of those near-integrated institutions which he can tactically afford to be out of; e.g., those that have to do with high culture, excluding educational centers. If he can sustain this tension, something may happen. The white man may want to help finance this withdrawal. LeRoi Jones need not feel guilty if some foundation gave him money to run Spirit House, as long as it wasn't something the foundation wanted to use against black people. That should be the attitude. I'm not for the love bit Baldwin is always preaching. Love is conditional. A man loves a man or woman, not a race or ethnic group. It is convenient to hate a group. A healthier situation is that of respect between groups and humanistic socialism within a nation. Maybe by love Baldwin means simply this respect.

At the moment, the function of literature in the South African context is in a state of suspension. Censorship, and laws against sabotage and terrorism are savage. Come the time of the open revolt, when we have been able to master the technique of distributing underground literature, a good deal of revolutionary poetry will emerge: revolutionary in the sense of its immediate goal and audience and the prerequisite mood of urgency. Those of us in exile will only continue to write out of the sheer inner compulsion.

The black man is in the majority in South Africa. The agony of waiting for "something" to happen here is of a different kind from the agony in the black American situation. The black American has to work toward the point where the white man will weaken, not out of any moral considerations but out of necessity. The black man in South Africa has to work toward breaking the white man. He needs to hate more than he is doing. Only after the revolution can he allow the civilized white to stay for the reconstruction. A small band of white political prisoners already qualify. Dennis Brutus writes the way he does because he has faith in the future: he can argue with himself, with his god, with his political destiny. Because he knows he must win even if posthumously. For this reason there is not the sustained desperate urgency in his or Kunene's published poetry that we find in black American poetry. In both cases we see a poetry we know we can continue to read even after the present state of agitation without feeling embarrassed.

Angolan and Mozambiquan poetry follows the same leisurely but intensely felt pace as that of South African verse. The bitterness, the pain, are all there.

When poetry can be a vehicle of revolutionary passion and ideas and at the same time be what the writer wants to say, and that as memorable speech, we have the "truest poetry." It can anticipate the historical moment of armed revolution, it can promote it while the conflict is in process, and it can stay on as ritual during and after the event. Southern Africa as the last bastion of racism will not be spared a holocaust. Man naturally wants to upset the status quo when it is irksome. If the load bites into his shoulder, and he shifts it to the other shoulder or moves it slightly to another and easier angle, he does so only when it is an enforced load. He must throw it off. Blood may be spilled as a result, but that is how new societies and nations are also born.

Someone may argue that I have no right to make violence seem necessary if I myself am not going to the front. But there are people who are braver and more capable of active army service. There are other capacities in which I can serve. Literary critics are not necessarily artistic writers at the same time. You don't have to go into active politics to show that you are certified fit to observe government critically.

Outside the areas of conflict arising from black-white attitudes is the area of internal politics in various independent African countries today. We have seen already that we are going to witness more military coups, assassinations, imprisonment under a preventive detention law, and so on. The African poet seldom criticizes power inherent in the executive authority of his own country in the same terms that he criticizes white power. In many cases he may not want to destroy the institution of authority but remove those who operate it. The poet comes from the same tradition of values as his leaders, whether they have abandoned such values or not. We see a mild attack on political corruption in Cyprian Ekwensi's *People of the City;* the most devastating unrelieved attack in Ayi Kwei Armah's *The Beautyful Ones Are Not Yet Born;* another, although in symbolic terms, in Camara Laye's *Dramouss* (translated under the title *A Dream of Africa*); Chinua Achebe's *A Man of the People* is a satirical but important treatment of the subject. I am interested here in Wole Soyinka's play, *Kongi's Harvest.* Particularly am I interested in him as a poet, a feature you cannot miss even in his plays.

But I want first to examine briefly the nature of power we see in independent Africa today. In his highly perceptive essay "Monarchical Tendency in African Political Culture,"[108] Ali Mazrui discusses the monarchic orientation of political power in Africa. Kwame Nkrumah, former president of Ghana, he points

108. Ali Mazrui, *Violence and Thought* (London: Longmans, 1969), pp. 206–230. Reprinted by permission of Ali Mazrui.

out as an example, was a Leninist czar. He held leftist ideas but struck a czarist pose in his presidential activities.

Professor Mazrui sees four elements of political style that constitute the monarchical tendency: first is the "quest for aristocratic effect," consisting of all the visible accessories of aristocracy like palatial splendor, ornamental attire, luxury cars, and "other forms of conspicuous consumption." Second, the "personalization of authority," which reflects a personality cult and sometimes makes the leader take a special title. Nkrumah called himself the *Osagyefo,* the redeemer. Another may take a name that is literally royal. Third is the "sacralization of authority," sometimes connected with the personalization element, sometimes not. Sometimes again, although rare in Africa, it may be the institution and not the person that is sanctified. "Indeed, the personality of the leader might be glorified precisely because the office lacks the awe of its own legitimacy." The fourth element in the monarchical style of politics is "the quest for a royal historical identity." This consists in the effort to reinstate a connection, real or legendary, with a glorious historical past. The ancient kingdoms of Ghana, Mali, Songhai (Nigeria), Malawi are examples. A leader can thus imagine himself to derive power from any of the ancient kings in his own region. In order to assert Africa's dignity, nationalists point to the ancient civilizations that flourished in areas like Benin, Zimbabwe, and other kingdoms.

Professor Mazrui goes further to show how the "cult of ostentation" grew out of the sense of individualism that already existed even in traditional days of cooperation or communal labor and ownership of land. Education and a money economy promote this cult today. African leaders, with rare exceptions like President Nyerere of Tanzania, often measure their success and importance by the material wealth they have amassed. And yet it is education and money, too, that today help the new generation to challenge the traditional sense of authority, both in themselves and in the leaders. There is ostentation and sense of prestige on both sides. The wealthy citizen and the wealthy leader get on very well with each other.

In addition to traditional ideas about the inviolability of the office of authority if not the authority as well, there is the imperial experience. Through colonialism Africans in countries of British influence came to revere the kings and queens of England. Ideas of royal splendor set in among African leaders. "Republicanism," Professor Mazrui rightly concludes, "is in a sense alien to the African style of politics." It was the arrogance of the French policy of assimilation that sent francophone blacks to traditional symbols, which in turn prevented French republicanism from rubbing off on the African's political style.

It is thus a paradox that in the process of a new state being born, the new nation should revel in the glories of the past. "Ancient kingdoms and modern presidents are then forced to share royal characteristics."

The sanctification of a leader's office, or of the leader himself, has always been a strong tendency in the making of new states. George Washington became both a historical and legendary name to the Americans in the days when he was creating a new state. He was referred to variously as "the great ornament of human kind," "originator, and vindicator, both patron and defender of the faith," "a necessary creation for a new country," "godlike Washington," and "a man standing on the border between human and divine," and so on.

Perhaps in new states people are still close in time to the demoniac autocracy of the saintly benevolence of traditional royalty. George Washington's white America has just come out of life under powerful English monarchs. In Africa we have just recently come out of such a life or have not yet shaken it off. Perhaps, too, in South Africa, where kings were defeated and chiefs have long lost the respect of the people, republicanism has a chance. Successive white regimes reduced chiefs to the level of glorified police, and in spite of the present government's attempts to restore the chief's authority and importance in the Bantustans, it will never be the same thing as in traditional times. And with at least 7 million out of the 14 million blacks (including Coloreds and Indians) living outside the Bantustans, it seems that monarchic tendencies, if they do emerge, will exist merely because of our sense of theater and as a comic show in the eyes of the proletariat.

We are not, in independent Africa, far in time from the oral praise poetry that is loaded with such hyperbole as in:

> Voracious consumer of the root and the branch;
> Descendant of Menzi! plundering till plunder is gone;
> Thou fount of Nohamba! drinking of which,
> I dropped down dead, and sunk into
> the shade of Punga.[109]

This is a praise to Senzangakona, Chaka's father and Zulu king. Nohamba was one of the first royal towns of the Zulu. Menzi is one who creates.

The Thonga of Mozambique have this to say about a king:

> Muhlaba Shiluvane, you are like the rhinoceros who seizes a man, bites him through and through, rolls him over and cuts him in two! You are like the crocodile which lives in water; it bites a man! You are like its claws; it seizes a man by his arms and legs, it drags him into the deep pool to eat him at sunset . . . you are on the top of the hills, you are like heaven which roars. . . . The lightning is like you, it is full of strength. . . . Your body is like the stone of gold. . . . You are like the grass in the road; when people trample on it, they crush it to the ground, but when the rains come, it grows again and covers the earth. . . . You are like the ostrich feather, the white one very white, or the red one of the bird which cries tswe-tswe, the bird called rivi, which adorns the chiefs! [110]

Ali Mazrui quotes the following, being a praise by Tawia Adamafio to Nkrumah (Adamafio was chairman of Nkrumah's Convention People's Party):

> To us, his people, Kwame Nkrumah is our father, teacher, our brother, our friend, indeed our lives, for without him we would no doubt have existed, but we would not have lived; there would

109. Willard R. Trask (ed.), *The Unwritten Song* (New York: Macmillan, 1966), I, p. 80.
110. *Ibid.*, pp. 87–88.

> have been no hope of a cure for our sick souls. . . . What we owe him is greater even than the air we breathe.[111]

Nkrumah was also said to be literally immortal.

> What monarchical republics of Africa have now been out to assert is the new doctrine of the divine right of founder-President. Nor is the doctrine entirely without justification in countries which have yet to establish legitimacy and consolidate the authority of the government. As Apter has put it, "the sacred characteristics become essential to maintain solidarity in the community." [112]

The sanctification of authority, as well as its personalization, Mazrui concludes, represents the climax of political power in Africa. The head of government or head of state then begins to symbolize "the soul of the nation." But the quest for aristocratic effect is seen not only in the executive authority but also in the lower strata of society. Often it is even the rank-and-file who insist that this effect should grace the show of power, however modest the leader himself might be or try to look.

> The aristocratic and kingly aspects of African styles of politics have deep roots, both in African traditions and in the total impact of the colonial experience. African conceptions of earned rewards, the spiritualization of ancestors, the quest for a historical identity, the assertion of cultural equality, the general desire for political glamour have all contributed their share to the monarchical tendencies in African politics.[113]

President Kongi in Soyinka's play *Kongi's Harvest*[114] is an archetype of the politician whose style shows monarchical tendencies. He lives in palatial splendor which he has arrogated to himself after putting away in preventive detention the Oba (Yoruba king). He has places named after himself like Kongi Terminus, Kongi University, Kongi Dam, Kongi Refineries,

111. Mazrui, *Violence and Thought*, p. 224.
112. *Ibid.*, p. 226.
113. *Ibid.*, p. 230.
114. Wole Soyinka, *Kongi's Harvest* (London: Oxford University Press, 1967). Reprinted by permission of the publisher.

Kongi Airport, and so on. He and his Secretary are thinking of counting years from the "Year of Kongi's Harvest." In a thousand years, the calendar will show "1000 K.H."; for the purpose of back-dating, BKH—Before Kongi's Harvest. In this way, the perpetuation of his name and the thrust of personality will be assured, at any rate until a new and hostile order emerges.

The beginning of the Five-Year Development Plan must be launched by the feast of the New Yam. This feast has religious significance: it sanctions the harvesting of the new yam crop. The Oba usually eats the biggest yam on this occasion. As he is in detention now, Kongi orders that he be released so that he can come and present the yam to the President at the dais, who will then eat it. "I *am* the Spirit of Harvest," Kongi tells his Secretary, who adds, "and a benevolent Spirit of Harvest." Earlier, he said of Kongi, "the Leader's image for the next Five-Year Development Plan will be that of a benevolent father of the nation"—an image that must be projected at the Harvest festival. "The key word is Harmony," says the Secretary. The President's retreat in the mountains, where he is now meditating and fasting, also has a religious aura.

Kongi has driven the old Aweri—the traditional clan of elders—from their seats and appointed in their places what he calls "members of the Reformed Aweri Fraternity." The traditional king is a god, and Oba Danlola refers mockingly to Kongi as "His Immortality."

The Reformed Aweri Fraternity, Kongi's creation, must obey him. "A conclave of modern patriarchs," the First Aweri calls them—"a kind of youthful elders of the state." The Fourth Aweri observes that Kongi would "prefer a clean break from the traditional conclave of the so-called wise ones." In order to justify their role, the new Aweri tell one another that their traditional counterparts were "remote impersonal"—features that "breed fear in the common man" and therefore necessary. The traditional proverbs, "the ponderous tone rhythms," the paraphernalia, and so on might be too cumbersome, but these "youthful elders" must have an image. They may complain about having been forced to fast because Kongi is fasting, but they need an image. They may regard Oba Danlola's office as "this reactionary relic of the Kingship institution," and may wish he were not alive. But they need him to maintain this traditional aura for the common man's consumption.

The Fourth Aweri says:

> I think I see something of the Leader's vision of this harmony. To replace the old superstitious festival by a state ceremony governed by the principle of Enlightened Ritualism. It is therefore essential that Oba Danlola, his bitterest opponent, appear in full antiquated splendor surrounded by his Aweri Conclave of Elders who, beyond the outward trappings of pomp and ceremony and a regular supply of snuff, have no other interest in the running of the state.

He is wrong about the Elders of course: they *were* interested in the affairs of state. But the Aweri have to justify their modern role; the Oba must acknowledge "the supremacy of the State over his former areas of authority spiritual or secular. From then on, the State will adopt towards him and to all similar institutions the policy of glamorized fossilism."

This new bunch of Aweri is pretty cynical about its office, about the length of speech that one of them should write for the President, even about Kongi himself. The Fifth Aweri suggests that, to persuade Oba Danlola, who is reluctant to cooperate at the feast by presenting the New Yam to the Leader, Kongi could grant those political detainees who have been condemned to death a reprieve.

> *Secretary:* You are raving. Kongi does not want the new yam that badly.
>
> *Fifth:* You are good at these things. Rack your brain for some way of getting him in the right mood.
>
> *Secretary:* You don't know how he hates those men. He wants them dead—you've no idea how desperately.
>
> *Fifth:* I do. But tell him he can kill them later in detention. Have them shot trying to escape or something. But first, demon-

> strate his power over life and death by granting them a last-minute reprieve. That's it, work on that aspect of it, the drama of a last-minute reprieve. If I know my Kongi that should appeal to his flair for gestures.

All this is likely to lead us to think that the Aweri and the Secretary are political clowns, with which Africa abounds; that they are performing these monarchical dramatics in order to entertain themselves, to laugh. They may also be reflecting Soyinka's sense of humor. But Kongi takes himself seriously all the way. He must retain a historical identity with the Oba, who is both a secular and spiritual leader; he must pretend to retain the institution of Aweri Elders in all its essence. Here is another bit of elevated flattery of the Leader from his Secretary, who is trying to get his superior to grant amnesty to those awaiting execution:

> It's all part of one and the same harmonious idea my Leader. A Leader's Temptation. . . . Agony on the Mountains. . . . The loneliness of the Pure. . . . The Uneasy Head. . . . A Saint at Twilight. . . . The Spirit of the Harvest. . . . The Face of Benevolence. . . . The Giver of Life. . . . who knows how many other titles will accompany such pictures round the world. And then my Leader, this is the Year of Kongi's Harvest! The Presiding Spirit as a life-giving spirit—we could project that image into every heart and head, no matter how stubborn.

If the Aweri and the Secretary are having a good laugh, alternately making serious and mock-serious statements about their own image-making antics ("Our pronouncements should be dominated by a positive scientificism"), Soyinka soon makes us rudely aware of the menacing forces at work in Kongi's power exercise. The father of Segi, the Leader's former mistress, has escaped from detention; and in the foolhardy act of returning during the feast, he is shot by security guards. Kongi is moved to say, like a king and priest of a fertility ritual:

> The Spirit of Harvest has smitten the enemies of Kongi. The justice of earth has prevailed over traitors and conspirators. There is divine blessing on the second Five-Year Development Plan.

> The spirit of resurgence is cleansed in the blood of the nation's enemies, my enemies, the enemies of our collective Spirit, the Spirit of Planting, the Spirit of Harvest, the Spirit of Inevitable History and Victory, all of which I am. Kongi is every Ismite.

Segi brings her father's severed head on a salver to the President, who is struck speechless with terror. Kongi's wrath is unleashed. In the epilogue (titled "Hangover") we see Oba Danlola and the Secretary trying to make their way to the border, but no comrades in exile.

Through the steady and grave pace of the Oba's speech, which is in verse, and that of Daodu's speech before the Leader, we are able to feel the pulse of Soyinka's indignation against this kind of power, power that takes on the trappings of a culture of which the playwright himself is one of the sons.

As Danlola is being pressured to present the New Yam to the President and thereby also make himself irrelevant as a King, he delights in taking his own time to prepare himself. When the Secretary tries to suggest that he need not appear so elaborately dressed, he replies with sarcasm:

> Then, my dear son-in-politics, this being
> The only way in which our dignity
> May be retained without the risk
> Of conflict with new authority,
> Let us be seen in public only as
> Befits our state. Not to add the fact
> That this is Harvest. An Oba must emerge
> In sun colours as a laden altar.

Introducing his grandson and heir, Daodu, to the Secretary, Oba Danlola says:

> Lately returned from everywhere and still
> Trying to find his feet. Not surprisingly.
> It must be hard to find one's feet in such
> Thin arrowheads. Daodu, before you
> Flaps the Big Ear of his Immortality.

In his brief speech at the feast, Daodu says:

> An impotent man will swear he feels the
> pangs of labour; when the maniac finally
> looks over the wall, he finds that there,
> agony is the raw commodity which he has spent
> lives to invent.

He goes on to say that he has brought his prize-winning yam. Let it be cooked, let the soup simmer in the pots, so that "the Reformed Aweri Fraternity may belch soundly instead of merely salivating, that we may hereby repudiate all Prophets of Agony, unless it be recognized that pain may be endured only in the pursuit of ending pain and fighting terror."

The play is orchestrated with verse praises for the Oba and for Kongi. The Carpenters' Brigade, another of Kongi's inventions, sings his praises. The Brigade is the equivalent of the youth groups one sees in several countries in Africa today, e.g., Young Pioneers, Youth Brigade, and so on. The Carpenters laud Kongi as "our father," "our mother," "our Saviour Redeemer, prince of power."

This is a modern monarchic style of presidential rule. The people sing adulation to a leader as king, god, savior, and so on, just as they did only yesterday, before the kings and later chiefs were stripped of their powers by white rule. We do not yet wield instruments of dissent as a citizen mass; most of the citizens do not care much about processes of government, because they do not understand them. And so heads of state entrench themselves and think they have a divine right to rule. If we can't bring down men like Kongi, who else but the army can and dare step in and take matters in hand? And even when the army has stepped in, there is no guarantee that the creative spirit, or the political spirit, will be able to function without a threat. Soyinka fell foul of a military regime in 1967, when he dared challenge the right of Federal Nigeria to march against the secessionist Biafra before exhausting civilized efforts to come to terms with the latter. He was kept in detention for just over two years, until October, 1969. Daodu and the Oba echo the voice of agony which previsions what Soyinka could very well say when he was later led into preventive detention.

He wrote two poems which found their way out of prison. In one, "Live Burial," he says:

> They hold
> Siege against humanity
> And Truth,
> Employing time to drill
> through to his sanity.[115]

So they "seal him live," thrilling "to hear the Muse's constipated groan."

Will he, the rebellious poet, like Antigone, dig up yesterday's corpses? Will he rake up the muck that comes with the birth of new times, new things?

Poems will always be made. Some, like those that are not written in a memorable diction and/or whose relevance and interests are confined to a tiny area of human concerns, are most likely to drop out of the stream of enduring literature. Fidel Castro says the artist who assumes that he is only creating for posterity is a victim of self-hypnosis.[116] He stresses that the artist creates chiefly for his contemporaries although his work may persist into posterity. "For the revolutionary," he says, "those goals and objectives are directed towards *the change of reality* . . . towards the redemption of man" (my italics). The ideals to change reality, to redeem man, sound rather too lofty for the poet. The revolutionary poet has to be that much of an idealist. As for changing reality, we can never hope to complete the task: which is why literature, the arts in general, will persist through the ages. But Castro does not want to lay down "principles of expression" for the creative writer: it would be an oversimplification, he says. He is content with the general rule that the

115. Wole Soyinka, "Live Burial," from *The New York Times* (June 7, 1969). © 1969 by The New York Times Company. Reprinted by permission.

116. "Words to the Intellectuals," by Fidel Castro, translated by J. M. Cohen. From J. M. Cohen (ed.): *Writers in the New Cuba.* Copyright Penguin Books Ltd., 1967, pp. 183–187. Reprinted by permission of Penguin Books Ltd.

artist must try to reach the people. He is prepared to accept that "all artistic manifestations are not exactly of the same nature. . . . There are expressions of the creative spirit that by their very nature are much more accessible to the people than other manifestations."

Indeed we now realize that the revolutionary poet, the poet with a sense of urgency that arises from a sense of mission, can pressurize the flow of his ideas and feelings along that single channel only so much and so long and no more, no further. There comes a point, surely, when there is nothing to be said that can be given a fresh view within the framework of one's mission. And I know from my own personal experience in South Africa that one suffers both mentally and physically from such sustained pressurization. It goes beyond the point of therapy when one feeds on the poison that is generated in oneself. What to do—write other and less emotionally exhausting lyrics or seek a synthesis in oneself between the urge for a singleness of purpose and the urge to open all of one's windows to let in other sounds of humanity? Talking within the context of our topic, I am sure Gwendolyn Brooks, Soyinka, Brutus, achieve this synthesis with superb skill—certainly in terms of range and accessibility.

In varying degrees, the newer Black Power poets, taken as a chorus or community of voices, show an orchestration that is most stimulating and elevating. I have already pointed out that in single poets we can see a diction that gives their revolutionary verse body and vibrates through the bones and the blood. I want to see later the cumulative effect of their individual poetry before I can answer for myself the questions I am asking about it. For now, the poetry does something to me as a collective voice, and the writers may well say that is all they want it to do, damn posterity. But *that* conceded, it is still not an adequate answer to the vanity that is in all of us—to persist into posterity. If one can do both, what is wrong with that? As I. A. Richards says, in the process of getting the poem "right" he communicates effectively. By the same token, it must endure into the future, because it will be remembered.

Poetry is not going to help us resolve social conflict. But through it we are going to see ourselves as we are and perhaps as we want to be; through it we are going to recite to one another our own selves. Especially when it is a chorus of voices we are listening to. That is really all we can hope for—a self-realization.

There are clearly two theaters of conflict and violence in Africa today: the kind in southern Africa, where we are faced with white fascism and its instruments of torture, and the kind we see in the scramble for power among the elite and between the army and the elite in independent Africa. We are much less ambivalent as writers about white fascism than about what I may call "black-white power," in which the black man has simply taken over the instruments of white power. It is sad to see us march against our own people with tanks and ammunition bought from a country like Britain which she refused to use against her own kith and kin in Rhodesia to liberate 4 million suffering blacks. We see little generals and colonels playing menacingly at war against their kith and kin in order to put into practice what they learned from the British at Sandhurst. "We know you're stupid enough to kill your own brothers; we never do that," I can hear the British say. These little men fail to see Rhodesia as a straightforward case of race politics: black rebels must be run to earth, jailed, humiliated before they can be called to Lancaster House for talks. White rebels can take what they want at any time.

Things are bound to get worse in these two areas of conflict. The more insecure we feel in independent Africa, the less we shall be inclined even to think collectively about the fascism of the Deep South of our continent. Already there is a hollowness in the protests and protestations we hear from time to time from the Afro-Asian bloc of the United Nations and from the Organization of African Unity.

Each area will evidently have to deal with its own local conflict, as is happening in Mozambique, in Angola, and must still happen in South Africa and Namibia. Censorship laws work havoc on the writer in these parts. He can only write freely in exile—a spiritual ghetto of its own kind, agonizing to reckon with. In independent Africa, censorship exists mostly in the writer's own mind and can therefore be more painful. We are seeing a new kind of abuse of power in Africa, new within the context of modern political styles. It remains to be seen what other writers in independent Africa will speak up like Soyinka, Achebe, Laye, Armah.

These conflicts give rise to the problem of refugees. I seek asylum in an African country. I have a profession and can practice it. I say I don't even want to be treated as an expatriate who is normally given allowances over and above his basic salary. I say I just want to work and be able to collect my thoughts and to contribute materially to the liberation struggle against South African fascism. That's all I want. They put me through the pipeline that is supposed to lead to an employment permit. If I am lucky enough to get one, fine. Later I am told that as I don't have a valid passport that will enable me to return to South Africa (sic!), my permit cannot be renewed. I've got to quit. Or else I'm told they are "Africanizing" jobs. And this doesn't include me. I've got to quit. When I quit, they replace me with a white expatriate, who is going to cost them much more than I did. It turns out that really they would rather their people were taught or advised by a white man than by a black man. Maybe because a white man represents power. But I can still move on and sell my services in a non-African country. What about the hundreds and thousands of black refugees who have little or nothing to sell by way of labor?

Some tell me, "Go back to your country and fight!" "What are refugees," I answer, "if they have not fled from something?" They laugh and continue to taunt me. One year, two years later, we all meet in Dar es Salaam or some other African capital, all of us refugees. *They* have fled from the wrath of the Frankenstein monsters they created, men like Soyinka's Kongi. That's it, you see, we shall meet in exile somewhere. Because we are all children of violence. It's here with us, *négritude* or not. Not even assassinations are a new phenomenon in Africa. We seem to be slow to liquidate quislings in liberatory movements; we don't seem to like doing it. But as in the early days, we go for those who ostensibly wield power and influence. And we are evading the truth when we blame some "agents of imperialism" for the violence we generate against our own people. Surely the Big Powers can collect a fat ransom on Africa any day or they can get their way in any deal with Africa without having to indulge in the messy business of killing off this or that leader.

We can learn the right lessons from traditional African humanism if we are prepared to recognize our brutal realities for what they are. People will continue to write poems which, to use LeRoi Jones's word, will *replay* the strains of conflict and other human realities by way of articulating what were hitherto the dumb lyrics of a people's inner music. Thus, to ask of what use poetry is, is to ask at one level what the human shout and cry are all about; at another level it is to ask what happened when the intellect took off on its own, and in so doing, tore the art of verbalizing off from its original moorings—the shout, the cry, the ballad, the praise, the epic. Of course, we shall be told that man needs to find a language today that will handle the complexities of the subconscious, of time, and so on. Imagery and symbolism do this adequately, I am sure, and they are basically as old as man's perception.

As I go on looking for the meaning of poetry, I hit upon this poem by Cuba's Fayad Jamis. He sums up beautifully for me what the voices from the whirlwind are all about. He calls it "Life."

Do you wish this poem to be only
the lilac's shadow the memory of the fountain
pure day drowning in my anguish?
Do you wish this poem only to speak in whispers
in the mid-afternoon
when sleep with its odour of sap enters the nests
and so many live things seem dead?
But now as you listen Spring bursts like a shell
and my poem has no lilacs or sleeping veins

but the sound of reality close at hand.
Myself I move and work and remove
old useless things and hear
my fellow-fighters' breath
and as I smoke this poem is born
and as this poem grows
Spring sings in my land.

You wish that only my silence spoke
and now my bones shout and my voice is not alone
and I tell you that night is beautiful in the window
and more beautiful in the sweat of men who
are struggling
in workshop and trench
at this moment when a white-winged star
is piercing the world's darkness.
For though you expect a lilac's shadow
to fall on the evening from my poem
you will see only my clenched fist fall and in
my verses
life will flower with all its fires.[117]

Let me clinch a few assertions. I have tried to focus on the concept of a black aesthetic only in the context of American political conflict because here it has been most consciously canvassed. I have not dared to answer categorically whether or not there is a black aesthetic in poetry. But I have attempted an examination of poetry inspired by rebellion against power or poetry that is itself an act of defiance. This kind of poetry is often a target of contempt among fanatic formalists. At best it is dismissed with a word of condescension. I have indicated that the subject matter of a poem itself does not distingish a "black" poem from a "white" poem. We need evidence that pertains to the fabric of the poem, including diction, rhythm or movement, and structure—to mention only the most obvious

117. "Two Poems," by Fayad Jamis, translated by J. M. Cohen. From J. M. Cohen (ed.): *Writers in the New Cuba.* Copyright Penguin Books Ltd., 1967, pp. 58–59. Reprinted by permission of Penguin Books Ltd.

features. Some Afro-American poetry shows a delightful synthesis of poetry as a state of mind and poetry as a powerful language—the synthesis of a language one feels compelled to use by force of political circumstance, and that which he *wants* to write because he is who he is. I have indicated that the ironic tension in a poem between what a poet has to express and the urge to communicate is an age-old one. The degree of this tension, I insist, makes for memorable language.

To the extent that some Afro-Americans are infusing the speech rhythms of their people into their verse and are seeking a meeting point between the people's poetry, which has existed since the language developed, and the poet's own individual voice—to this extent, the black American is moving toward a black aesthetic. The black experience already includes religious worship, dance, indigenous idioms in music, a native metaphor, and symbolism in the spoken language. Side by side with conventional Western theater, for which several Afro-American playwrights are creating plays, is a black theater that is experimenting with idioms that echo an African heritage. In the verbal art of poetry, where the *individual* sensibility is hammering out something, we are on uncertain ground. At this personal level the poetic form is elusive, skittish, eccentric, adventurous, but still valid. All we can be sure of is the communal consciousness expressed in poetry, the communal cry of pain, of joy, of anger, of survival. And here we are back to subject matter.

In Africa and the Caribbean one can hardly talk of a black aesthetic, except in indigenous languages and life-styles. Poetry written in European languages in these areas must, however, necessarily be affected by local cultures. And we must try to tune into these cultures if we want to understand the given literature. We need not be anthropologists, but we can get to know a people's way of life and thought that are related to the literature we are contemplating.

People who sneer at free verse seem to ignore the plain fact that more and more people in the diverse English-speaking world are using it and making meaningful poems. They are utilizing the built-in rhythms of the language. There is a kind of poem that says, in effect, that the situation is bad. It can thus, as in an epic or ballad, replay a race riot or a court trial in which racism is loaded against a black prisoner in fresh and memorable language. Such a poem would *have* to rely on the vitality of the language. At this point I can say that I would very much like to see a revival of black poetry in the world of the ballad, the epic, and the long narrative poem (satirical or otherwise), treating of contemporary life. A modern poem that comes to mind immediately is "Song of Lawino" and its sequels by Uganda's Okot p'Bitek, a fine and popular example. There is another poem that soaks in reality and explores the meaning of a bad situation for one's community and for society as a whole. There is yet another kind of poem whose *sole purpose and no other* is to exhort its audience to burn and pillage and to plunder and kill. It takes for granted several things: that the audience is of the same political persuasion, that it understands the political situation very well, and that its emotional responses are ready to be triggered off. It compels an immediate reaction. My view is that if we want to "say it like it is" to an audience, spoken prose is the best and most reliable because it is the most direct method, and we need not waste our time composing a poem. We can also compose a song saying the same thing with much better results. The first two modes of poetic expression have been used from time immemorial, and there will always be audiences who will be moved by such poetry.

Within the range of the second mode I have mentioned, several things are possible in the process of expressing one's emotions. Once a man has produced a poem, he no longer has control over it: it becomes public property and is available for new interpretations at every stage of our consciousness, whether within the writer's own generation or later on, because with the passage of time we know more, experience more, and develop new interests and new techniques of coping with life's problems. Interpretative methods run out of fashion when we have no further use for them, but they may be restored if conditions require it. For this reason, although ideally we would like our works of art to survive us, we must realize that every generation needs its own kind of artistic fulfillment for which our works may be quite irrelevant. It so happens that if we have taken the trouble to penetrate reality, with intellectual and emotional honesty in relation to that immense pulse called life, *and at various levels,* our poetry is more likely than not to vibrate beyond our present condition, even while it is inspired and informed by that condition.

The man who writes a poem with only one purpose, e.g., to evoke literally a single emotion, is assuming a terrifying responsibility and taking monstrous chances; he is using a suggestive language which, when it appears in print, he cannot control, and it can be interpreted in ways other than he intended.

On the other hand, the man who says poetry is "an act of language" and smugly stops there, is deliberately shutting out of his consciousness the riches of human experience. He is most likely to exclude from his anthology the latest poetry of, say, LeRoi Jones—an excruciating assault—because it appeals to responses other than the love of language. Using a work of art means interpreting it by applying it to our lives, finding correspondences that relate to our lives so that it can enrich our lives. And the fanatic formalist should realize that if poetry is to revitalize language, the poet must choose the form he feels best exploits his ear for language, always bearing in mind that he has an unspoken contract with his readers. Although a poem is understood it may not move a reader, but it must be understood in order to be appreciated.

There is a divine arrogance (for lack of a better epithet) that all artists share. But there is an arrogance that poets often share with certain modern painters and modern classical musicians (more than novelists or playwrights). It is an arrogance that has something to do with the idea that as long as you are *expressing yourself,* to hell with the contemplator, spectator, or reader. This is a monstrous twentieth-century abuse of the worthy nineteenth-century Romantic poetics of self-expression. I have no time for these modern artists, whatever their virtuosity in handling their instruments.

The whole problem is that the creators of elevating, imaginative literature generally, their critics, and their educated readership—the only people who buy their goods—create their own aesthetics which whip up and down the vertical plane of enlightenment, and the aesthetics remain as an intellectual activity—a kingdom unto itself. The only thing that will help distribute the benefits of literature on a wider horizontal plane is universal education, once we can identify the chaff and sawdust that hinder present-day educative processes. Even so, education to understand literature is rather special. It seems that one of the very few times literature strives to reach the underprivileged strata of society is when it is concerned with sociopolitical causes, with the suffering of man as a victim of power. Because the creators of such literature care desperately about man, they must engage his sensibilities, using the simple and basic proposition that man re-creates a poem or a story for himself as he reads.

This accounts for the almost desperate efforts writers make to perform their works orally for large audiences and to write a poetic language that will excite, move, and elevate ever larger segments of the public by speaking to both their plight and their resilience and survival—such efforts should not be belittled or sneered at. Meantime, we must realize that the theater is still the most direct, the most accommodating, and the most tolerant medium of the imagination for both instruction and entertainment, once it is shorn of all the clutter, frills, and fanfare that go with stagecraft, and once it is freed of the dirty economics that promote it.

African Literature: What Tradition?

It all started when Africa was shanghaied into the history of the West in the late nineteenth century. What were we coming into?—a long line of continuity going back some 9,000 years since the civilizations of the great river valleys of the Nile, the Tigris and Euphrates, the Indus, and the Hwang-ho had launched man on a long intellectual quest. We had been discovered by an aggressive Western culture which was never going to let us be. Nor could we cease following the neon lights —or has it been a will o' the wisp? Time will tell. Perhaps Hegelian historical determinism will have it that it is as it should be: how could Africa be left out of it all indefinitely?

And so here I am, an ambivalent character. But I'm nothing of the oversimplified and sensationalized Hollywood version of a man of two worlds. It is not as if I were pinned on a rock, my legs stretched in opposite directions. Education sets up conflicts but also reconciles them in degrees that depend on the subject's innate personality equipment. It seems to me a writer in an African setting must possess this equipment and must strive toward some workable reconciliation inside himself. It is an agonizing journey. It can also be humiliating to feel that one has continually to be reassessing oneself with reference to the long line of tradition he has entered—the tradition of the West. How else? I have assimilated the only education the West

---

This essay originally appeared in the *Denver Quarterly,* II, No. 2 (Summer, 1967), pp. 36–68.

had to offer me. I was brought up on European history and literature and religion and made to identify with European heroes while African heroes were being discredited, except those that became Christians or signed away their land and freedom, and African gods were being smoked out. I later rejected Christianity. And yet I could not return to ancestral worship in any overt way. But this does not invalidate my ancestors for me. Deep down there inside my agnostic self, I feel a reverence for them.

The majority of writers in Africa, I venture to say, are attached in a detached manner to one indigenous religion or another. They are not involved in its ritual, but they look at it with reverence. When, in their full consciousness, they have found themselves Christian—which can often just mean baptized—they have not adopted churchianity. Because our whole education system in Africa has been mission-ridden right from the beginning, and the white minister was supposed by the government or commercial or school-board employer to know the "native," you had always to produce a testimonial signed by a white church minister when you were applying for a job. Not even black ministers could speak for you. If you wanted to go out for further studies, you knew where to find St. Peter. The black minister himself required testimonials from one of his white brethren, never from another black minister. So we called ourselves Christians; we entered "Christian" on the line against an item that asked for it on all the multiplicity of forms, just in order to save ourselves the trouble of explaining and therefore failing to go through the gates. In independent Africa, we are luckily able to trust fellow blacks who vouch for us and others. And you can almost see the Christian veneer peeling off because it has nothing to do with conscience.

The Negro sculptor in Africa south of the Sahara (one must always make a distinction between this and North Africa with its predominantly Muslim culture) has always felt the tug of tradition acutely. It will be a tribal or ethnic tradition, not an all-African one. Sculpture has always been related in some subtle way to the handicrafts—all three-dimensional products. Like handicrafts, sculpture, mostly in wood, was a utility article. Wooden carvings have been used as shrines. They were practically all the same within groups. There would seem to have been little or no individuality in the works, because they had to conform to ritual. But then the African artist enjoyed the creative moment in itself, even if it produced the same kind of article over and over again. The figures at the shrine might rot or break, and similar ones would be made. And there have always been so many ideas to be expressed around any particular cult that a great variety of figures emerged. Again, others worked in metal they cast themselves. The close tie with tradition is only natural when one considers the sculptural medium itself.

In a story of his childhood, *The Dark Child,* Camara Laye of Guinea describes a scene in which he is watching his father, a goldsmith, melting his metal.[1] As the boy sits looking on, he realizes that gold-smelting in his father's workshop is a magical operation that "the guiding spirits could look upon with favor or disfavor." It is a traditional ceremony or a shorter version of one. All the apprentices present stand or sit motionless. Only when the gold is a fluid can the silence be broken. His father's lips move all the time, uttering secret incantations, which is why the goldsmith would rather perform the operations himself instead of the equally efficient apprentices. A black serpent that moves in and out of the workshop always comes and coils itself up under a sheepskin during the preparatory stages.

It is the custom, he reports, "to keep apart from the working of gold all influences outside those of the jeweller himself." Because "the working of gold, besides being a task of the greatest skill, is a matter of confidence, of conscience, a task which is not undertaken excepting after due reflection and experiment." "I believe my father," Laye proceeds, "never entered his workshop except in a state of ritual purity." After the preliminaries, he then begins to beat out his trinkets.

In one novel, Camara Laye tells of a blacksmith who attached

1. Camara Laye, *The Dark Child* (London: Collins, 1955).

the same spiritual value to his axe-making as the author's father did to his craft. It didn't matter how many axes he turned out; what did matter was the whole creative process.

Traditional sculptors and other craftsmen did not produce for the exhibition gallery or salon. The artist, as distinct from the craftsman who sold his wares, was patronized by the king or other important personage in the clan or village. With the disappearance of much traditional authority which has given way to Western patterns, and with the relatively lower economic status of the rulers who have survived, the village artist has all but gone out of the scene. A few still continue, but try to organize themselves in terms of modern marketing methods. This must of necessity be achieved at the expense of the original spiritual impulse that produced such an impressive variety of figures and masks that breathe a mysterious life one feels is comprehensible only to those who appreciate and understand the impulses that operate within the particular cults. You will find these *objets d'art* across West, Central, and East Africa.

South Africa has produced little sculpture. The people here seem to excel in pottery, grass-weaving, and in indigenous architecture of round grass-thatched houses and decorative painting on the floors and on the exterior of the walls. The designs are effected with a cow dung mixture on the floors and earth colors on the walls. As Africans have been driven into municipal "instant" houses (if one may call them that) the decorative art has proportionately diminished. Apart from this kind of work, and the Bushmen rock paintings, the latter of which rather express a group attitude than an individual one, two-dimensional art such as drawing and painting is a Western innovation in Africa.

Today African artists go to university schools of fine art to learn painting and sculpture. The artist is put through the history of European art and its techniques, and he cheerfully (so it would seem to the contemplator) churns out painting and sculpture that are African only in theme. Always hovering over him is this formidable traditional sculpture I have mentioned earlier. Should he imitate it? He does not take part in traditional ritual as a committed participant. So when he tries to imitate the art of his forerunners, he can only recapture the form, never the original spiritual impulse. The result lacks life. His environment demands other techniques, the things he wants to say are of a different nature and order of complexity. But he does not want to feel that he is neglecting tradition. The masks around him stare at him and seem to tell him he cannot ignore them if he wanted to. Indeed everywhere around him are armchair intellectuals and politicians who want to feel smart at openings of art exhibitions or other cultural occasions—people who are always telling him and the writer and the musician to return to the source, to preserve African culture. Just as if you only needed to pluck the fruit from the culture and can or pickle it. Yet why should he not be worried by tradition? He works at a time when Africa is becoming conscious of itself. If the African is being liberated politically, why should the artist, the writer, the intellectual in general, not want to decolonize his thinking?

There are those artists who talk themselves into the mood for taking something from tradition but are technically incapable of it; there are those who never even bothered about it and are quite happy for their work to be judged in relation to the long line of continuity we have been pushed or dragged into—that of Western tradition. I am reminded here of an art group in a workshop in Salisbury, Rhodesia, which has expressly stayed away from art school or art class methods and has begun to paint and sculpt under the direction of a British artist. He never imposes any theories or techniques on them. The results are astounding. We may yet see tradition accounted for, not necessarily directly through the art that stands at some remove in the past. It may sneak in from the area of verbal arts and craftwork. Who knows?

African music is not in much danger of losing sight of tradition. Everywhere indigenous music is being sung in the villages or being popularized in the cities through the use of such instruments as the guitar and one kind of percussion instrument or another. In South Africa, much traditional music is being tried out on small jazz ensembles. The jazz here is certainly developing in a direction away from the West because of the influence of traditional rhythms. This is specifically an urban development.

By far the larger part of Africa is still traditionally minded in varying degrees. The whole dialogue around tradition is an intellectual one. The parents of people of my generation, although they may be urbanized, are still close to tradition. They worry a great deal about the way in which we break loose at one point and ignore some elements of tradition. Each time an African mother sends a child to high school, it is like giving birth to him all over again. She knows she is yielding something. Dialogue between her and the child decreases and eventually stays on the level of basic essentials: our needs, our family relations, family life, which must continue more or less normally, whatever else around us may progressively be reduced to abstractions or gadgets. It is no less excruciating for the young man who stands in this kind of relationship with his parents. But he can reconcile himself to it—the very educational process that wrenches him from his moorings helps him to arrange a harmonization within himself.

The parent will often moan and complain to him about the awkward distance he has reached away from tradition. But it is never a reprimand; it is an indulgent complaint. Because, I think, the parents are always aware that this whole business of education does not of itself engage you in an activity that expressly subverts the morals of the family, the clan, or of the tribe. They are aware of the many situations around them that require an education to cope with them. The benefits of tradition are abstract, and the parents' own thinking has not been stagnant while the whole landscape around them has been changing, while the white man's government has been impinging on their way of life over several decades. And the benefits of a modern education are tangible, real.

I have always asked myself what it is in one's formal education that leads to the rupture, to the ever widening gulf between one and one's parents and one's community. You recognize the alphabet, then words, and then you can extract meaning from many sentences in a row. With that shock of recognition, words leap into life in front of you. They set your mind on fire; longings and desires you would never have known are released and seem to whirl around in currents that explode into other currents: something like what you see in a glass flask of water that you have on a naked flame to observe the movement of heat in liquid. From then on, one must not stop. Yet it is not something one can take for granted in an African context, because to start at all is not inevitable: education is not compulsory, and the financial cost of it is immense.

In your higher education, you assimilate patterns of thought, argument, and so on from an alien culture in an alien language; they become your own. Of course you cannot help using your African setting as your field of reference; you cannot help going out of the queue of Western orientation now and again to consult those of your people who are not physically in it. You try to express their philosophy in a European language whose allegory, metaphor, and so on are alien to the spirit of that philosophy: something that can best be understood in terms of allegory and metaphor that are centered heavily on human relationships and external nature. All the same, you are in the queue, and you belong not only to an African community but also to a worldwide intellectual or worldwide economic community, or both. This is why communication becomes difficult, sometimes impossible between your people who are still not tuned into Western intellectual systems and yourself. Your mind operates in a foreign language, even while you are actually talking your mother tongue, at the moment you are engaged in your profession. You try hard to find correspondences and you realize there are only a few superficial ones: you have to try to *make* most of them. In the pure sciences, which are universally applicable, the correspondences are numerous; there is no problem.

Indigenous languages that have only recently become literary, that is, only since the church missions established presses in Africa, seem to have relied more and more heavily on the spoken word, so that gesture, facial expression, inflection of voice became vital equipment in communication. Language became almost a ritual in itself, and metaphor and symbol became a matter of art and device. Metaphor became a sacred thing if it had descended from usage in earlier times; when an elder, in a traditional court case, prefaced a proverb or aphorism or metaphor by saying, "Our elders say . . ." his audience listened with profound reverence. Notice the present tense in "our elders *say*. . . ." Because his elders would be the ancestors, who are still present with us in spirit. You can imagine what confusion prevails in a modern law court when a witness or the accused operate in metaphor and glory in the sensuousness of the spoken word quite irrelevant to the argument at hand. Ask any magistrate or prosecutor or lawyer in a differentiated Western-type society whether they find a court trial a sensuous activity, and hear what they say. Even the rhetoric that a lawyer may indulge in is primarily a thing of the brain rather than of the heart. In African languages, activities overlap a great deal, and there are no sharp dividing lines between various functions.

All that I have said so far has been an attempt to indicate the relative distances between tradition and the present—some shifting, others freezing, some thawing, others again presenting formidable barriers. And we are living in a situation in which the past and the present live side by side, because the past is not just a segment in time to think *back* upon: we can see it in living communities. We need to appreciate these distances if we are to understand what the African writer is about. He is part of the whole pattern.

There is a considerable body of oral literature that is now increasingly being translated into English and French. Most of it is praise poetry, epic about historical heroes, gnomic verse, all which were recited by talented speakers on festive occasions. Naturally, it loses much of its power when recited in translation.

Swahili, which is basically a Bantu language with a considerable in-fusion of Arabic vocabulary, is a dominant language in East Africa. The Swahili poet was often a religious teacher as well. He instructed his people on the Islamic faith and conduct and exhorted them to keep it. Here is a Swahili poem, "The Poor Man":

The poor man knows not how to eat with the rich man;
When they eat fish, he eats the head.

Invite a poor man and he rushes in
licking his lips and upsetting the plates.

The poor man has no manners, he comes along
with the blood of lice under his nails.

The face of the poor man is lined
from the hunger and thirst in his belly.

Poverty is no state for any mortal man,
It makes him a beast to be fed on grass.

Poverty is unjust. If it befalls a man,
though he is nobly born, he has no power with God.[2]

The praise poem is one of the most favorite forms of oral poetry. Here is a praise to Shaka, king of the Zulus in South Africa who established a powerful military empire during the earlier part of the nineteenth century:

He is Shaka the unshakable,
Thunderer-while-sitting, son of Menzi.
He is the bird that preys on other birds,
The battle-axe that excels other battle-axes.
He is the long-strided pursuer, son of Ndaba,
Who pursued the moon and the sun.
He is a great hubbub like the rocks of Nkandla
Where the elephants take shelter
When the heavens frown . . .[3]

Another poem called "Song for the Sun . . . ," from the Fang people in Gabon, near the Republic of Congo:

The fearful night sinks
trembling into the depth
before your lightning eye

2. Ulli Beier, "The Poor Man," from *Swahili Poetry* by L. Harries (Oxford: Clarendon Press, 1962). Reprinted by permission of the publisher.
3. Translation by A. C. Jordan, *Africa South* (Capetown, 1956).

and the rapid arrows
from your fiery quiver.
With sparking blows of light
You tear her cloak
the black cloak lined with fire
and studded with gleaming stars—
with sparking blows of light
you tear the black cloak.[4]

Finally, a praise to a Yoruba king:

No one can try to fight you.
One who shakes a tree trunk shakes himself
. . . .
You are like death
who plucks a man's eyeballs suddenly.
You are like a big ripe fruit
that falls on a child at midnight.
. . . .
Whenever you open your mouth wide,
you swallow a hero.[5]

Although it may sound bloodless in cold print and more so in translation, one can sense in this oral poetry the necessity to place a premium on the spoken word. The facial muscles, gestures of the hands, the posture of the body, and the inflection of the voice all came in to reinforce the spoken word as a vehicle of meaning with its own aesthetics.

We have no kings to sing praises to in our age. And our heroes? Either they are in some demagogue's dungeon as political prisoners and therefore no fit subject for jubilant lyricism, or, if they are free, they look too unreal. Their gains cannot be assessed in

4. Ulli Beier, "Song for the Sun That Disappeared Behind the Rainclouds," in O. Trille (ed.), *Au Coeur de la forêt equatoriale* (Paris: Les Editions du Cerf, 1945), p. 151. Reprinted by permission of Ulli Beier and Editions du Cerf.

5. "The timi of Ede," from *African Poetry,* edited by Ulli Beier (New York: Cambridge University Press, 1964), p. 42. Reprinted by permission of the publisher.

unequivocal terms such as an ancient hero's own physical prowess or his genius to inspire it in others. Not only is there a subtle and swift interplay of light and shade on the faces of our heroes who are free that confuse us, but we the contemplators are also changing. It is almost as if death had to arrest the energy of a hero, freeze it, nail it down in some niche of Time so that we can label it with an epitaph before the hero has a chance to do something unheroic or mock heroic.

What are the writer and the painter, who are using techniques that are alien to this tradition expected to learn from it? Can one express the sentiments we read in the oral poetry I have quoted from in a language like English or French which operates on the assumptions of its own music, so different from that of our indigenous languages? The writer who works in his own mother tongue, if he is dealing with eternal verities and social realism, has no such basic problem. His idiom is a living one, spoken by the people he is writing about. He can struggle to find a vocabulary to deal with experiences that are peculiar to the whole encounter with the new technology, philosophy, etc. The chances of success are not remote.

Those of us who write in the metropolitan languages know that we have abandoned the direct route leading from tradition, which is the mother tongue, for the more intricate and perilous one of interpreting experience in a language and genre that belong to a historical tradition outside our own origins. It is a perilous commitment. The inept novelist in this category usually writes the anthropological novel in which the action is halted, so that he explains the workings of African custom. Or he advertises Africa as the symbol of his lost innocence, deploring, even as he drives in his car, the replacement of the path of naked feet by tarmac. Sometimes this rediscovery of Africa is genuine, particularly for the writer who was educated abroad. In some cases, it is an intellectual projection by which the sophisticated writer tries to locate himself in relation to the past and the present. Quite clearly—and this is one of the perils—these writers are directing their material to a Western audience whom they think they need to inform about Africa. They fail to synthesize exposition, narrative, idea, feeling, and style into a work of art.

Another peril for us lies in the fact that we have to be judged in terms of the tradition in which we write—English or French or Portuguese. Publishing houses of the Western world must needs by guided by the literary standards (or whims) of a non-African reading public. The African reading public is almost negligible in proportion to its extra-African counterpart, although, with educational advance, our indigenous audience must grow. African publishing houses are now emerging and beginning to take on material that would be regarded an economic risk outside the continent, however high its literary merit may be. It should not be difficult to imagine a story or play written out of an African or Scandinavian or German or Rumanian or Russian experience which, however good, would not go beyond local interest.

There is the inept Negro poet who writes his praise song to Jomo Kenyatta, President of Kenya:

. . . .

Kenyatta
    Je clame ton nom
    la main sur l'oreille
    Je me tourne vers le Nord
        le Sud
        l'Est
        l'Quest

Jomo
    Ils ne savent pas
    Mais ils sauront
    Que tu es
    Racine de Baobob millénaire

Ils ne savent pas
    Mais ils sauront
    Que t'habit l'Esprit
    des trois Fleuves

Nil
Niger
Congo.[6]
. . . .

It is quite clear here that the poet is trying to imitate the oral tradition. And it simply won't work. And I think we might take a lesson from the fact that there are very few literary ballads today in the European traditions. The above poem does not even pretend to be literary.

Whenever this identification with one's African past is a negative reaction—a revulsion against Europe, the poet's diction simply fails to carry felt thought. Gabriel Okara, a Nigerian poet who writes some of the best English poetry of Africa, lapses into this kind of mockery of the white man's apparently artificial laughter:

In your ears my song
is motor car misfiring
stopping with a choking cough:
and you laughed and laughed and laughed.

The white man's is "ice-block/laughter and it froze your inside/froze your voice your years," where the black man's is

the fire
of the eye of the sky, the fire
Of the earth, the fire of the air . . .
the fire of the seas and the
river fishes animals trees
and it thawed your inside
thawed your voice, thawed your
ears . . .[7]

and so on.

6. Cheich Ndao, "A Jomo Kenyatta," *Présence Africaine,* LVII, p. 124. Reprinted by permission of the publisher.

7. From Langston Hughes (ed.), *Poems from Black Africa* (Bloomington: Indiana University Press, 1963), p. 83. Reprinted by permission of the publisher.

Yet when the same poet allows himself to respond fully to such disparate notes as those of a piano and those of an African drum, the true poet in him will not permit him to oversimplify the effect they have on him. He writes:

Then I hear a wailing piano
solo speaking of complex ways
in tear-furrowed concerto:
of far away lands
and new horizons with
coaxing diminuendo, counterpoint,
crescendo. But lost in the labyrinth
of its complexities, it ends in the middle
of a phrase at a daggerpoint.
And I lost in the morning mist
of an age at a riverside keep
wandering in the mystic rhythm
of jungle drums and the concerto.[8]

The sledgehammer effects in the following lines from a Ghanaian poet leave me numb, almost senseless:

Our God is great
Who dare deny it?
Our God is great
Powerful and dark
Peering through ages
Healing, killing, guiding along.

Our God is black
And like any goddamned god
Guiding when loving
Killing when angered.

Our God is powerful
All-powerful and black
And like all deities

8. Gabriel Okara, "Piano and Drums," in Gerald Moore and Ulli Beier (eds.), *Modern Poetry from Africa* (Harmondsworth: Penguin, 1966), p. 122.

Our Godhead likes blood
Whether it be blood of Isaac or ram
Our God likes blood . . .

The poet concludes by saying that he will stay with his God. It is not the poet's preference of his God to a Christian or other God that I take offense to. It is rather his outright certainty about the necessity of a God and the way He is supposed to operate that I cannot accept:

Slow to anger when fed fat on yams
And of great mercy when suckled on blood.[9]

Who knows for certain the things we deserve and those we do not and God's role in the whole business?

A more convincing statement on a similar subject comes from a compatriot of the same poet. He imagines that the spirits of the ancestors come to find their living children

Shuffle their sandalled feet to the same rhythms,
They heard the same words of wisdom uttered
Between puffs of pale blue smoke:
They saw us,
And said: They have not changed! [10]

Of course we have changed to some extent. But the latter poet will at worst set us thinking about our traditions, and taken as a whole his is a fine poem. The former poet closes his book and leaves no room for discussion. And yet both are concerned about tradition.

One never seems to be able to talk of tradition in Africa without mentioning *négritude*. This term was an invention of Aimé Césaire, a poet of Martinique and fellow student of Léopold Sédar Senghor in the Paris of the 1920's and the 1930's. They found themselves cut off from their African roots and assimilated into French culture. They decided that from then on

9. Frank Kobina Parkes, *Songs from the Wilderness* (London: University of London Press, 1965), p. 16. Reprinted by permission of the publisher.

10. Kwesi Brew, *The Shadows of Laughter* (London: Longmans, 1968), p. 52. Reprinted by permission of the author.

their poetry should reflect the truth about the Negro and not what the white colonial master would be pleased to hear. Their poetry took on a strong spirit of protest against colonialism, which was dehumanizing the Negro, or turning him against his own people if he was educated. The poetry evoked images of ancestral spirits, shrines, sacrificial ritual, masks, naked bodies, blackness in general, and so on. *Négritude* became thus not only a slogan which was to instill a sense of self-pride and dignity into the black man, but a mode of artistic expression the writers believed should come to signify a characteristic Negro one. As a social concept, it came to be thought of as the sum total of African values.

At its worst, *négritude* has inspired, particularly in lesser minds, verse like

> Ecoute:
> I la-i la la-i la
> I la-i la la-i la
> Que Dieu garde Oumara Kelba,
> Qu'il le fasse toujours plus fort,
> Toujours plus riche et plus puissant
> I la-i la la-i la
> I la-i la la-i la
> Que la terre entière adore mon maître
> Quaï . . . Quaï . . . Quaï . . .[11]
> . . . .

It has inspired romantic nonsense like what we get from Léon Damas of Guyane in the Caribbean:

> Jamais le Blanc ne sera nègre
> Car la beauté est nègre
> et nègre la sagesse
> car l'endurance est nègre
> et nègre le courage
> car la patience est nègre

11. Francis Bebey, "Qui es-tu?" *Présence Africaine*, LVII, p. 14. Reprinted by permission of the publisher.

et nègre l'ironie
car le charme est nègre
et nègre la magie
car l'amour est nègre
et nègre le déhanchement . . .[12]

The poetry of *négritude* origin may also falsify the image of Africa by representing it as a symbol of innocence, purity, naked beauty, human decency. Africa is not an innocent continent. My violent hates and my passion for vengeance for the brutalities my people have to endure do not make me European in the least or less African. Some *négritude* verse leaves one rather worried by its elusiveness. Take Sédar Senghor's poem "New York." It has vivid images on the surface which lead one to think there is some solid, tough realism beneath "the nights of insomnia," "hygienic loves," "nylon legs," "legs and breasts that have no smell," "artificial hearts," etc., that he associates with Manhattan. Then he goes into Harlem. Because there are Negroes here, he imagines "a green breeze of corn" springing up "from the pavements ploughed by the naked feet of dancers," "bottoms wave of silk and sword-blade breasts," "streams of black milk." Then he pleads:

New York! je dis New York, laisse affleurer le sang noir
dans ton sang
Qu'il dérouille tes articulations d'acier, comme une
huile de vie
Qu'il donne à tes ponts la courbe des croupes et la
souplesse des lianes.[13]

—let black blood flow into New York, so that it may rub the rust from the city's steel joints, like the oil of life, so that its bridges may bend like buttocks and creepers.

Negro blood, buttocks, and creepers—I love them all myself. New York may well need them. But I am sure Dakar, Kampala,

12. Léon Damas, *Black-Label* (Paris: Editions Gallimard, 1956), p. 52. © Editions Gallimard 1956. Reprinted by permission of the publisher.

13. Léopold Sédar Senghor, *Ethiopiques* (Paris: Editions du Seuil, 1956), p. 56. Reprinted by permission of the Georges Borchardt Literary Agency.

Brazzaville, Nairobi, Salisbury also need them; indeed any city in the world that has ghettos has to forgo whatever qualities the people of such ghettos could contribute to their human constitution. Yet more important still is the fact that Harlem is a ghetto and still a portion of Manhattan. No observant person could deny that there are survivals of African culture among American Negroes; that somehow, because Negroes have been segregated for over 300 years and have therefore had to create areas of self-sufficiency, they have not disappeared in the so-called American melting pot. Even when they are integrated, they remain like pebbles in a mouthful of rice. You don't have to sort out the pebbles or chew the rice. If you do, your teeth will get what they want. Some American Negroes say they refuse to be integrated into a "burning house." Others again want nothing so badly as to be absorbed by or with the whites. Some have no hope that an active outgoing identification with their African past can be of any good. Economic and political integration must often mean a compromise of some portion of one's identity. All such paradoxes are often missed by the poetry of rejection or of acceptance. And neither facile rejection nor facile acceptance makes good poetry.

I agree fully with Aimé Césaire's attitude that the *négritude* movement must be seen in its historical perspective: as a phase that was necessary if the African had to restore his sense of dignity that colonization had undermined. And when one reads Caribbean French and Spanish and American Negro poetry, one realizes how *négritude* must essentially and originally be a non-African Negro phenomenon. The communities that produce this poetry have been alienated in a way Africans have not been—alienated without a hope of physically recovering their African roots.

American Negro poets of the Negro Renaissance of the 1920's and 1930's like Claude McKay, Countee Cullen, Langston Hughes, Arna Bontemps once used to be called the "Rhythm Boys" because, as an intellectual response to the white man's rejection of the Negro, the poet began to feel nostalgic about his

African past and the rhythm of its drums; naturally he could not imagine more than the African songs that

> beat back into the blood—
> Beat out of blood with words sad-sung
> In strange un-Negro tongue—
> So long,
> So far away . . .[14]

To Claude McKay (incidentally a West Indian by origin), Africa comes vaguely as

> The song that fills me in my lucid hours,

and

> The spirits' wine that thrills my body through,
> And makes me music-drunk, are all yours.[15]

To Arna Bontemps,

> Darkness brings the jungle to our room:
> The throb of rain is the throb of muffled drums.[16]

What is Africa to me? asks Countee Cullen—

> Copper sun or scarlet sea
> Jungle star or jungle track,
> Strong bronzed men, or regal black,
> Women from whose loins I sprang
> When the birds of Eden sang? [17]

14. From Langston Hughes, "Afro-American Fragment," in Langston Hughes and Arna Bontemps (eds.), *The Poetry of the Negro* (New York: Doubleday, 1949), p. 102. Reprinted by permission.

15. From Claude McKay, "Heritage," in *Selected Poems of Claude McKay* (New York: Bookman Associates, 1953). Reprinted by permission of Twayne Publishers, Inc.

16. From Arna Bontemps, "The Return," in Langston Hughes and Arna Bontemps (eds.), *The Poetry of the Negro* (New York: Doubleday, 1949), p. 115. Reprinted by permission of Harold Ober Associates, Inc.

17. From Countee Cullen, "Heritage," in Countee Cullen, *On These I Stand* (New York: Harper & Row, 1947). Reprinted by permission of the publisher.

I think we find *négritude* poetry at its best, even within the limited framework of its protest, when it flows from the more genuine and more lasting and more excruciating sense of alienation that we find in the Caribbean islands. There is a dignity of anger here that enriches the diction. Césaire writes:

. . . .
Ma négritude n'est pas une pierre, sa surdité ruée contre
la clameur du jour
Ma négritude n'est pas une taie d'eau morte sur l'oeil mort
de la terre
Ma négritude n'est ni une tour ni une cathédrale
elle plonge dans la chair rouge du sol
elle plonge dans la chair ardente du ciel
elle troue l'accablement opaque de sa droite patience.[18]
. . . .

His *négritude* is no deaf stone that reflects the noise of the day, he says. It is no spot on the dead eye of the earth; it is no tower or cathedral. But it dives deep into the red flesh of the soil, into the flowing flesh of the sky, piercing the weight of oppression with its erect patience.

Césaire writes in another poem, "Africa":

. . . .
the forgotten days which walk always among the twisting
shells among the doubts of the regard
shall burst upon the public face among the happy ruins!
In the plain
The white tree with helping arms outstretched will be
like every tree
a tempest of trees in singing foam and sands
the hidden thing shall climb again the slope of
slumbering music
a wound of today is a womb of the orient
a shuddering which rises from the black forgotten fires,
it is

18. Aimé Césaire, *Cahier d'un retour au pays natal* (Paris: Présence Africaine, 1956), p. 71. Reprinted by permission of the publisher.

the ruin risen from the ash, bitter word of scars
all lithe and new, a visage
of old, bird of scorn, bird reborn, brother of the sun.[19]

The image of Africa here is being evoked to enable the alienated Negro to come to terms with his humiliation.

A poet of Haiti, Jacques Roumain, presents another aspect of the theme of Africa in his piece "Guinea." Here he employs the old Haitian belief that Guinea (in West Africa) is a kind of Negro heaven to which all Negroes will go in death. They will rest here in eternal comradeship:

It's the long road to Guinea
No bright welcome will be made for you
In the dark land of dark men:
Under a smoky sky pierced by the cry of birds
Around the eye of the river
the eyelashes of the trees open on decaying light
There, there awaits you beside the water a quiet village
And the hut of your fathers, and the hard ancestral stone
where your head will rest at last.[20]

The Cuban poet Nicolás Guillén reconciles his "Two Ancestors": They are two shadows haunting him . . . the two dream in the night; they sigh together, lifting their heavy heads: after all, they are both of the same size under the high stars: black greediness and suffering, white greediness and suffering, white fear and black fear . . . they both dream, weep, sing. . . .

If you are an African and feel alienated in Paris or London or Lisbon, you can go back to your home. If you still feel alienated, you are among your people and can pick up some of the threads where you left off. You may of course be dragging threads that were cut twenty yards away from the ends you are holding, centuries away from the source. Even this homecoming

19. From Gerald Moore, *Seven African Writers* (London: Oxford University Press, 1962), p. x.

20. From *An Anthology of Contemporary Latin American Poetry*, edited by Dudley Fitts. Copyright 1942 by New Directions Publishing Corporation. Reprinted by permission of New Directions Publishing Corporation.

has its own complications. This is how Lenrie Peters, a Gambian, feels about it. Although it vaguely suggests a *négritude* spirit, it does not derive directly from the movement.

> Too strange the sudden change
> Of the times we buried when we left
> The times before we had properly arranged
> The memories that we kept.
>
> Our sapless roots have fed
> The wind-swept seedlings of another age.
> Luxuriant weeds have grown where we led
> The virgins to the water's edge.
>
> There at the edge of the town
> Just by the burial ground
> Stands the house without a shadow
> Lived in by new skeletons.

Sometimes it is for him like coming down on a parachute:

> . . . the warm earth
> Reaches out to you
> Reassures you
> The vibrating interim is over.
>
> The violent arrival
> Puts out the joint
> Earth has nowhere to go
> You are at the starting point
>
> Jumping across worlds
> In condensed time
> After the awkward fall
> We are always at the starting point.[21]

For the American or Caribbean Negro, it has to remain an intensive intellectual projection. But we can still appreciate

21. From Lenrie Peters, "Homecoming," in Gerald Moore and Ulli Beier (eds.), *Modern Poetry from Africa* (Harmondsworth: Penguin, 1966), p. 79. Reprinted by permission of Lenrie Peters.

négritude as a necessary social movement for the assimilated African, with varying degrees of emphasis. It has to enter into a frank and intensive dialogue with present-day politics, economics, education, etc., which we share with the other tradition. As a poetic movement, which Senghor tried to make as relevant to Africa as it has been for the Western Hemisphere, it is petering out. In independent Africa, the myth will no longer suffice. In any case, it was conceived by an elite, its poetry remained always a private dialogue among the elite about a specifically elite experience, since most of Africa is still closely in contact with living traditions.

The best poetry in Senghor's list of achievements is that which reflects the meeting point between rejection and acceptance. It is quite plain to us now that "New York" must have been a time-piece. As President of Senegal, he has, in real life, to reconcile very many more things than he had in his writing years. Even then he was already arranging inside himself this meeting point. He writes:

> . . . J'ai rêvé d'un monde de soleil dans la fraternité de
> mes frères aux yeux bleus,

and ends the same piece:

> Demain, je reprendrai le chemin de l'Europe,
> chemin de l'ambassade
> Dans le regret du Pays noir.[22]

I have spoken at length on the various poses African, Caribbean, and American Negro writers adopt in relation to the past: poses that are also the measure of the writers' protest against colonization, material and spiritual. The main link here is of course the Negro's color, and an Africa that is no more just a continent of misty swamps and jungles and distant drums, but one of real people who stand ten feet tall as independent communities.

22. Léopold Sédar Senghor, *Chants d'ombre* (Paris: Editions du Seuil, 1945), pp. 75 and 77. Reprinted by permission of the Georges Borchardt Literary Agency.

I began by indicating the pull of tradition which we cannot ignore. I have suggested that tradition in Africa is not, as in the Western world, made up of centuries or eras telescoping into one another. Rather, it consists of various patches of landscape with several common features such as ancestral worship, the humanism that consists in a moral emphasis on social relationships, respect for elders, and so on. It is the entry of the white man into our midst and the colonial experience that have now made us think of these common features and a possible common source. For this reason many poets have written of Africa as a unified entity. It is the will to conceive a common past and the ideal of a common destiny that has inspired the Pan-African movement. Tradition lives alongside the present, and so we the writers commute between these worlds. We want to reflect our immediate present in foreign languages so as to reach a wider audience, and in one way or another we feel the desperate need to come to terms with an ever present past.

It is as if we wanted to account for tradition, because it won't let us be. After all, our parents, still custodians of tradition, sent us to school, to university, and the community they belong to also feels somehow, without expressing it, that it has a claim on the benefits of our education. It wants us to share its concerns in a practical way. And so our writing becomes the very process by which we communicate with tradition, define ourselves by defining it. We do this by creating plots for our fiction in which characters are engaged, some in an identification with tradition, others in breaking away from it, others again in trying to reconcile in themselves and in their fellow men these opposing forces.

There is the fictional story of the priest who feels humiliated after he has been arrested by a white administrator for refusing an appointment as chief. He goes back to his people convinced he is the arrow of God, meant to punish them for their sins. He delays the sign they need for the harvesting of their yam crop. To prevent the yams from rotting as a result of this delay, the people give in to the argument presented by the Christian church among them that they can harvest the crop without incurring the wrath of their traditional gods if they only bring some to the church for a Christian blessing. The priest becomes mentally deranged.

Another story tells of a young schoolteacher born into traditional beliefs who tries to bring about harmony between two hostile communities—his own and the Christian one across the river. He falls in love with a Christian girl, whose sister died a reject because she absconded from her father's house to join circumcision school. The teacher's dream was to unify all the village communities into a political movement strong enough to stamp out white rule. This is frustrated by the final cry among his people: How could their teacher betray them? How could he work for the togetherness and purity of the tribe and then marry a girl who was not circumcised? How could he do this to them?

A secret society to whose principles the teacher is bound by an oath decides to try him and to give judgment about his desire to marry the girl. Hostility remains. The river between continues to signify the line between the irreconcilables that often characterize a colonial situation, in which nationalism becomes an inevitable growth. In independent Kenya, the setting of the story, as in the rest of Africa, there is at present a kind of truce between the Christian God and traditional gods. The conflicts are seldom acted out in public dramatic terms as we have in the story I have recounted. The drama is now a silent, private one—in individuals and family groups—which is still waiting for a novelist to explore.

A novel of Guinea tells of a white man who has been rejected by his own kind. He decides to go into the African king's service. A native tramp offers to lead him to the south where he can wait for the king's visit and petition him. The tramp sells him to the aged local ruler in the south without the white man's knowing it. Each night, a young girl is sent from the old ruler's harem to sleep with our man. Because each night he smells the same perfume as with the first visit, our man does not realize that the ruler is sending him a different girl every time. Why all this abundant hospitality? The ruler is old and impotent and wants children. After a period we must assume cannot be less than nine months, our man is taken to the ruler's palace. There, in an enclosure, he sees the wonders he has performed: a large brood of colored children milling about quite gleefully. He is stricken with shame—the Christian-European kind. So when the king arrives, our man cannot face the moment for the petition. In the throes of guilt, our man even imagines a radiance about the king's person. But the king urges him to come and present his petition.

The white man has sought to identify with African tradition, and attains this state only after a rude shock—the recognition that to be initiated he has to be purged of the guilt complexes he has brought from another culture.

These, then, are some of the themes by which some African writers try to probe their traditions and account for them. Sometimes the dramatization of the black-white encounter is used as a means in the probe; sometimes events resulting from the encounter and therefore not requiring the appearance of white characters in the narrative. Sometimes the writer maintains an attitude of detachment; sometimes he makes it quite clear that he prefers traditional to Western culture.

It is impossible to speak on any subject concerning Africa without concluding with a big "but" or "however," which is necessary when one comes to speak of the South African scene.

A good deal of oral poetry has come down to us in Bantu languages, dating back to the fifteenth century. The earliest idyllic poetry gave way to the epic, composed and recited around heroes like Shaka of the Zulus, Moshoeshoe of Basotho, and the Xhosas of the Cape Province. The epic mood easily adapted itself to the theme of the black-white encounter of the eighteenth and nineteenth centuries—this time, a bloody encounter. It became protest epic in which the black hero was eulogized and the white one disparaged and abused in turn.

As everywhere else in Africa, this is a form that cannot yet be worked into the English or French language to deal with present-day major concerns.

There is another area of the encounter—an intellectual one

centered in mission schools. When the wheels of the mission presses started to turn, particularly when Africans established their own journals, a good deal of protest verse was composed and written in the three main Bantu languages. Of course the English verse form, which was imposed on these languages, made for artificiality, although metrical rhythm and rhyme were absent. Who knows how we would have written it if the Latin script were not introduced? The point is that when we began to write Bantu we were at the same time entering the Western line of continuity, bringing with us tons of protest material, gallons of vitriol, bags of peas for shooting, and a long satirical leer on our faces; and the languages were not wanting in ammunition with which to throw our equipment into this new tradition.

In 1884, we hear a poet say in Bantu:

Some thoughts till now ne'er spoken,
Make shreds of my innermost being;
And the cares and fortunes of my kin
Still journey with me to the grave.

I turn my back on the many shams
That I see from day to day;
It seems we march to our very grave
Encircled by a smiling Gospel.

Deriding Christians for kneeling when they pray, another poet says of hymns:

Which they sing in praise of the King,
Proclaiming Jehovah and Christ:
How strange to us that they turn to Him their buttocks,
Albeit proclaiming Him King! [23]

Toward the end of the nineteenth century, tribal life was fast breaking down as a result of mining enterprises and the rise of cities that were absorbing Negro labor, and as a result of the uprooting of whole communities by successive white govern-

23. Translations by A. C. Jordan, *Africa South* (Capetown, 1956).

ments that were herding us into rural and urban ghettos. The rural reservations with 5 million Africans, although forced to live in ethnic divisions, are in a state of perpetual change because of the labor force that moves between town and country. The writers here work in Bantu and, because of constant censorship from the government, produce idyllic verse and prose which must never portray the Negro as a man aspiring to political freedom.

The 3 million Africans who live as farm laborers on white people's farms are utterly unproductive intellectually, as can well be imagined. It is the 7 million Africans who live in towns and cities who have produced the most important and sophisticated writers in South Africa, using English as their medium. It is significant that except for two very well-known authors, we are all exiles living in Europe, the United States, and Africa.

The breakdown of tribal life prompted writers at the turn of the century and in the early 1920's to produce historical romances that implicitly sang the glories of our military past, of tribal cohesion, and of humanism. One such romance is *Chaka* by Thomas Mofolo, which is a classic in Sotho. Another is Solo Plaatje's *Mhudi.*

We gradually became committed to city life and, although rejected by the white man who wants only our labor, we have recognized the advantages of detribalized urban life. And the more we were dispossessed, the more intensely we came to value the family as a unit, communal living, and social relationships in conditions that were working against cohesion of any kind. We continue to observe family and communal ritual where birth, death, marriage, etc., are concerned, and speak our vernacular languages to those who understand us, English to those who do not. But we writers do not create a philosophy out of our Negroness. How could we, when in fact the white man has never let us forget we are black? It is the more immediate, excruciating reality that our poetry and prose are preoccupied with: the daily struggle for existence; ghetto living; frustration of ambition in the professions; the laws that make it imperative for us to account for movements any time a policeman stops us, and to carry an endless number of permits to leave one town and enter another; irksome separate entrances and exits at public places; the endless irritations attendant upon the sheer mechanics of black-white relations on any working day; police terror; police torture; house arrest; banishments; jail life which has ceased to be a shameful experience for a Negro, although harassing, and has become an initiation to adulthood; the pointless, meaningless loss of life; the banning of political action; deprivation of human dignity; the hate and the physical violence that the situation generates on both sides of the color line right from the age when we become aware of our color difference.

There are certain ways of escape of course: the music, the dance, and other forms of intensive creative activities. It is a fugitive culture that stays on all the more stubbornly for that. In the midst of it all, as the poet Dennis Brutus says:

> Somehow we survive
> and tenderness, frustrated, does not wither.
> . . . .
> boots club on the peeling door.
>
> But somehow we survive
> severance, deprivation, loss.
>
> Patrols uncoil along the asphalt dark
> hissing their menace to our lives.
> . . . .
> But somehow tenderness survives.[24]

This is our reality. The bother about tradition becomes to us only an intellectual concern. We feel it is something deep down there inside us. It is aroused only when we see it undermined in ourselves and in others, sometimes by the white man, sometimes by our own fellow blacks.

Night to Senghor and the poets who extol blackness is "plus véridique que le jour"; he says again, "Nuit d'Afrique ma nuit

24. Dennis Brutus, *Sirens, Knuckles, Boots* (Ibadan: Mbari Publications, 1963). Reprinted by permission of the author.

noire, mystique et claire, noire et brillante"; Césaire says, "la nuit peuplée de soleils et d'arcs-en-ciel." In his revolt against the violence of colonization, Césaire says:

> gémir se tordre
> crier jusqu'à une nuit hagarde à faire tomber
> la vigilance armée
> qu'installa en pleine nuit de nous-mêmes
> l'impureté insidieuse de vent.[25]

This is symbolic of the difference between a South African and Senghor. The night of Africa . . . my black night . . . the night of ourselves . . . night teeming with suns and rainbows. . . . Yes, these are poets who are in love with night. But for me night spells violence, police raids, screams. When I was a boy I became afraid of mountains and darkness because I was fully exposed to the terror they concealed while I wandered in search of cattle and goats. In the city, the night had other terrors for me. The South African writer is always searching for daytime. But this is no value judgment of either Senghor or the South African writer. I suspect when conditions do allow me to sit back and reflect more necessarily upon tradition, we in South Africa will find it is laced with just this suffering. I suspect that because the white ruling class is forcing us into traditional ethnic groups in an attempt to frustrate nationalism of a non-racial kind, when one day we decide on a pilgrimage to the source if we shall ever need to do that, we shall find it poisoned. How can one give a correct forecast about such things? While I am prepared to stake a lot on the survival of African humanism and the social relationships it informs, Emerson's voice keeps sounding back of my mind: "There are no fixtures in nature. The universe is fluid and volatile. Permanence is but a word of degrees." Again I look out to the north of us and see a new dimension of traditional reference in independent Africa.

Is the South African experience just another "myth of the

25. From Aimé Césaire, "Grand Sang sans merci," in *Ferrements* (Paris: Editions du Seuil, 1959), pp. 23–24. Reprinted with the permission of The Third Press–Joseph Okpaku Publishing Company, Inc., New York.

wounded Adam"? I don't know about the Adam. I do know a lot about the wound. And that is no myth. It is not impossible to give artistic expression to the cry and the anger and the hope. When the impulse to write kicks you in the pit of your stomach, you don't wait for the day you won't need to be bitter. Nor is bitterness inherently anti-art. Obviously, the two-dimensional stimulus-protest pattern will not do. But the very art of writing becomes a way of trying to cope with bitterness and anger.

Everywhere in Africa we shall for a long time to come continue to commute between tradition and the present. We shall be the vehicle of communication between the two streams of consciousness as they exchange confidences, knowledge, wisdom and dreams. The image of Black Orpheus conceived by Jean-Paul Sartre in which he dramatizes the black man searching for his Eurydice in the *négritude* underworld as it were is only part of the story. Because not only is the African present seeking out the past, but the past is seeking out the present. Of course Sartre did imply as much when he said a time would come when Africa would not need the *négritude* slogan. My own empirical attitude toward experience tells me that as a South African product I have to attend more urgently and first to the defense of human dignity.

The Fabric of African Cultures

The music floats in the night across the vast complex of African townships (or "locations" as they are called in South Africa). It is heard in all parts of this black metropolis because it is a loud and robust music. The singing dancers—all young men and women and boys and girls—stamp it out on the street each night for a whole month before a wedding until it sounds as if the musicians were trapped in a sunset-to-midnight orgy. The friends of the prospective groom and bride come and join in the dance and song. And so the theme of the music unfolds.

Mother-of-someone,
Come out and see:
here's a son-in-law,
he brings rain
and cold.

Sister, daughter-of-someone,
you go
to the home of strangers;
do you truly
desert your mother?

Come out and see
your daughter's gown;

This essay originally appeared in *Foreign Affairs,* XXII, No. 4 (July, 1964), pp. 614–627.

our bride
she's wrapped in silk.

You're so fair,
girl, so fair:
What had you to do
with such a coalblack
groom?
What had you to do
with me,
my girl?—
you found me in such rags.

Come my love,
let's run away
to shanty town,
tin-and-sack town,
let's run away
and lose ourselves
in shanty town.
The girl said No-no,
my Ma will come for me
Pa will kill me.
I'll go alone, then,
I'll find another bride
and lose myself
in shanty town.
No, don't go,
my love,
I won't come
but don't go.
And I went to shanty town
and broke to pieces-pieces
the heart of my beloved.[1]

The second lyric quoted above, unlike the first, tells the story of delinquency. There is a ring of urgency in the words. And as

1. Translated by the author from original Sotho lyrics.

the moon goes down, as if poised for a slow-motion hurtle behind the horizon, the musicians disperse. Tomorrow night again, they will sing. And here the city boy and girl have come in at a certain point of cultural continuity, a continuity that is being lived by country folk. The music is still intact; only the lyrics are drawn from city life.

Somewhere else in a dance hall a jazz combo is creating music; music taken from American Negro jazz and hammered out on the anvil of the South African experience: slum living, thuggery, police raids, job-hunting, shifting ghettos, and so on. The penny whistle takes the key melody, with bass and drums keeping the rhythm. On and off the sax weaves its way through the penny-whistle notes. The musicians grope their way through the notes, expressing by this improvisation the uncertainty and restlessness of urban life which rejects the Negro: its expectations, its violence. They play in order to escape from the pain of rejection and to assert their human dignity.

Those who dance to this music are also caught up in the tangle. They also improvise, although this is not immediately important. But there is something distinctly physical about their dance idiom, the way in which the bodies move—physical in a way the European idiom is not.

And so an urban culture has evolved. It is an escape route for a people on the run; but it is the only virile culture in South Africa, beside which the derivative and fragmented one of the whites (English and Afrikaans) looks sterile; it is something that sustains the black man.

There is another kind of music. This is the four-part choral music composed by Africans. And it is celebrated at annual *eisteddfods* where schools and adult choral societies compete. Some of the music is pastoral, full of nostalgia about pastoral tribal life. But much of it talks of freedom, exhorts people toward unity; it is about passes and liquor raids and police terror. This music has stood the test of time and does not follow fashions as pop music does.

Among the 4 million Africans who are now urbanized, there are several who maintain links with their people in the country, because they are relative newcomers in the towns. There is also a large population of female domestics who live on employers' premises and are in constant touch with their country folk. They are highly sophisticated, dress smartly in pay-while-you-wear clothes, but are not involved in the rough-and-tumble existence of location people. They carry back to their "reserves" transistor radios and gramophones, concertinas, mouth organs, town gadgets and foods, and new-style clothing. Those who envy them go to the towns to look for work, or allow themselves to be recruited for mine labor. The system of migrant labor is thus consolidated. The intercourse between town and country is thus established and maintained. Family life is broken in the process. But the human traffic keeps moving, like droves of ants, with a tragic inevitability. The lives of the 5 million Africans in the rural areas have consequently been disturbed. The land does not hold much for them anymore. The members of the family who have gone to the towns will send money when they can and when they have not been swallowed up by urban life. The Christian church, the school, the occasional mission clinic and hospital exert an influence of another kind.

Then there are the 3 million Africans working on white people's farms as labor tenants. They have, like the town folk, cut their tribal moorings, and owe no allegiance to a chief. Here cultural life seems to turn around in circles, finding no nourishment from either rural or urban life. Something about these people hangs in suspension, as if waiting for a fulfillment, the energy for which they are incapable of generating.

Any visitor who sees an urban African smartly dressed in American-style clothes, who sees him go to a cinema, read comics and paperback thrillers (as well as the English newspapers), who sees him collect jazz records—in short, the visitor who sees him live in town like one who is committed to it, and lives by its assumptions, may think the African has wholly surrendered his traditional values to an urban life that is a bad imitation of the "white" way of life. The townsman may well have done this. Indeed, if he was born in town, there is nothing to surrender; he merely takes his place in the scheme of things.

But there is a definite line of continuity in African cultures which acts on individuals and groups like the string by which a kite is held to the ground; it tacks and weaves and noses up, a toy of the wind while it remains up there; and yet it responds to the continual tug the boy gives it toward the ground. Again, the stresses and tensions and segregated existence of South African urban life have the effect of evoking the traditional African sense of community so that the individual draws strength from the group. The wedding ceremony itself is a mixture of civil, Christian, and African customs. Many more people come to the wedding feast than have been formally invited; the relationships between aunts, uncles, fathers, and mothers maintain a hard but acceptable African code during the negotiations for the bride and during the wedding celebrations. In the midst of all these, receptions are held in dance halls and a jazz band is hired for the occasion.

At funerals family relationships also follow an African code. Each night for a whole week before the burial of the deceased, relatives, friends, and acquaintances gather in his house to sing hymns, speechify, always in praise; they drink and pray. And altogether it is turned into a social occasion. A few days after the burial, relatives busy themselves with the washing of the bedding in the whole house. A year later, the widow will shed her black mourning, and she is then permitted by custom to put on any color of dress. Birth and the child's "coming out" (of the house) are also causes for get-togethers and a "little tea-and-cake." These are age-old customs taken from tradition and given an urban form.

Always Africans gravitate toward one another, even in the towns. A European suburb always looks dead on weekends. Most likely the inhabitants have gone out for a "little quiet"; or they are at the sports grounds; or they have gone picnicking. Although they may be thrown together in public places, it seems to be regarded as an unfortunate necessity. Africans, on the other hand, swarm the streets on weekends, just walking about and visiting. There is a continuous din in our areas: radios are switched on full blast. And even in this melting pot that is urban life, human beings matter more to us than things. We are not always, like Europeans, trying to master things, conquer or tame our setting. Formal education throws up individual talent which in turn, side by side with a money economy, builds up an individualism that creates problems unknown in traditional societies, where the welfare of the group took precedence over that of the individual. It is because of this, perhaps, that African writers, artists (who now do not serve group religious interests as the traditional sculptor did), teachers, doctors, occupy a special place as individuals in relation to their fellow men.

Worship in the so-called established churches, but particularly in the "separatist" or independent churches, has taken on a theatrical-revivalist character, and it is now clearly a pleasurable rather than a painful experience. There is a striking similarity between independent churches in Africa and their American Negro counterparts. Furthermore, belief in one God has reinforced in the African mind his reverence for and trust in ancestral spirits rather than exorcised them.

When I was a boy in a slum "location" of Pretoria in the 1930's, we were taught African ways of behavior at home: to take something with two hands from a grown-up; to curtsy while receiving something from an adult if you were a girl; never to occupy a seat while a grown-up stands; never to drink water before an adult if one was sent to fetch him some; never to sit in the company of adults or take part in their conversation; to allow the eldest child to take the first pick of anything given to the children to share, and to make the others follow in descending order of age. As much as city conditions allow, the family is still regarded by us as the center of society that must hold, whatever else may crumble around us. Our people take strong offense if a relative, no matter how distant, comes to our neighborhood and goes away without calling on them.

These are the broad elements of the "African Personality" that we can be sure are common to most of our societies on this continent: the place of the extended family in the social structure; the sense of communal responsibility; the tendency to gravitate toward other people rather than toward things and places; reverence for ancestral spirits; audience participation in entertainment activities. For the rest, we are all ambivalent personalities, switching from one form of response to another as we find convenient. Think of the educated African trying to concentrate on his private studies for a university degree in his house amidst loud street singing and dancing; think of the "been-to" who comes back home with an American or European wife whom he has then to initiate (or decline to do so) into the unending maze of relationships running through his extended family. This ambivalence is part of the "African Personality," and its nuances defy the politician's definition of the concept. Perhaps it is the artist, the writer, the musician, the actor who will reveal it for us—even that portion of it that lies in our ambivalence.

All this should be a warning to those Africans who think of a culture as an anthropological thing that belongs in the past and must be reconstructed as a mere landmark or a monument; the here and now of its struggle to come to terms with modern technology, with the confrontation of other ways of life, must give as valid a definition to our culture as its historical past. When one sees the granite monument that Indian culture and civilization are, and what a barricade against change they have been through the years, one begins to wonder if after all the African is not at a greater advantage for being able to absorb and contain the shock of change—if one can say this without justifying and approving the ruthless battering down of much of his culture by overzealous Christian proselytizing.

The most recent laws that have serious consequences for cultural growth and self-realization in South Africa are the Bantu Authorities and Bantu Education Acts. The former provides the government with an instrument for splitting African communities into ethnic groups, and through the latter it has devised a system of education that trains the African to serve his ethnic group on the assumption that his people must not be given weapons whereby they can compete with the European. The perverted logic of it is that this provides an opportunity for the black man to live his own culture (meaning obviously tribal culture) and saves him years of frustration which lie before him if he tries to make a living in what has already been pegged as white man's territory, and in a society that disowns him. This of necessity means an inferior education and undermines the advance Africans have made in producing a considerable intellectual force that is now making itself felt in the politics of resistance. This law supplements ethnic grouping in breaking the back of African nationalism, which has built up over the last fifty years to the point where inter-tribal marriages are commonplace and tribal divisions, particularly in the towns, are a thing of the past.

Whatever happens, it is quite clear that the proletarian culture will continue to gain strength if only as an unconscious defiance against the process of fragmentation.

II

Everywhere in black Africa one sees two main types of urban communities: the type represented by Johannesburg, Brazzaville, Dakar, and Nairobi on the one hand, and that typified by Lagos and Accra on the other. In the former category we see distinctly segregated black and white communities. The institutions in European areas are usually geographically or economically or legally inaccessible to the Africans, except the elite. So the Negroes are thrown on their own resources: they make their own music, create their own fun, borrowing what they want from European technology and art. Life is invariably much more vibrant, robust, and full of zest in these Negro ghettos than in the white areas, whose culture must be derivative and linked with the metropolitan centers, wriggling away without direction, like a lizard's tail cut off from the body.

The capitals of English-speaking Africa, on the other hand, are solidly African in atmosphere, if not wholly in architecture.* Before independence, whites here also shut Africans out of their

* One should strictly speak of *certain* English-speaking capitals and *certain* French-speaking cities, especially in Islamic West Africa. There is a self-confidence here one does not find in cities like Nairobi, Lusaka, Abidjan, Dakar, and so forth. The rural scene in Africa is changing, but it is in the capital cities, where Western styles are more prevalent, that we see the ambivalence because of new economic and social goals. At another and more general level, it does not matter whether the new or up-and-coming elite is French- or British-oriented; the complexities of cultural choice are equally excruciating.

so-called government reservation areas, but lately have come to realize that they were shutting themselves in. The West Africans have developed their "high-life" music and dance, as have South Africans their "kwela." There is a tremendous amount of self-confidence among English-speaking West Africans because British indirect rule left much of their traditional culture intact. But they have a high regard for British educational institutions, of which they are products, and a traditional distrust for American education. The encounter with more and more Americans through the Peace Corps and research students may have the effect of at least preventing the youth from adopting anti-American slogans and labels, and this in turn demands that they establish their relationships with Americans and British independently within the limits of current anti-West group attitudes. This is particularly so because British educators and administrators have played no mean role in instilling this distrust of American education, and it can therefore be outgrown. Certainly revulsion is setting in against Western educational institutions in general. There are paradoxes here: one is that while the British have wanted, through indirect rule, to guarantee their subjects cultural independence, they have tried to prejudice them against the non-British institutions of the West; another is that the longer it takes for the communities under British influence to revolutionize their curricula in secondary school and university to fit African political and socioeconomic aspirations, the louder Western institutions are renounced. Indeed the renunciation comes mostly from university students and not from the elite or the huge civil-service class that has emerged from a British education; the educated African does not collect *objets d'art,* and neither the artist nor the writer can hope for an audience among these groups for a long time to come. Their solid African-ness expresses itself in other ways.

African intellectual activity is derivative, because traditionally we did not analyze and formulate intellectual systems. Painting also is largely a foreign tradition. And the West African who comes out of art school, which is without exception part of a university, finds he has to do something desperate to relate to his immediate environment, in order to rid himself of the European influences that have been imposed upon him by his mentors. Because he has come into a line of continuity in a European tradition, and his people have no painting tradition apart from rock paintings that reflected a stylized group attitude, the student artist has no way of knowing what influences are bad and which will advance his work. His best course, then, is to relate to the monumental tradition of wood and bronze sculpture that tends to overwhelm him.

His problem here is to use this tradition in such a way as to recapture not just the image but also the original impulse that produced it; and this, on impossible terms: society's needs have changed to some extent; the chiefs who once patronized this religious traditional art have lost their power or are no more. But the very continuity of his people's life and its organization at deeper levels is sufficient for a real artist to draw his material and styles from. Those who have already begun to do this are but a negligible number.

The English-speaking novelist, poet, playwright in West Africa is very much an individualist. He is little influenced by his next-door neighbor, the French-speaking Negro, who demands that a black man's writing should give expression to the African's revulsion against European culture and re-assert his own people's cultural values—that it should follow a program. Yet Ghanaian poets like George Awoonor-Williams* and Kwesi Brew, the Nigerians like Chinua Achebe (novelist), Wole Soyinka (playwright), John Pepper Clark (poet)—to mention only representative names—show in their work the unconscious urge to come to terms with their traditional life, to determine their position in relation to it. Stylistically, all these fall in the British tradition. They are, however, giving English a fresh and new usage.

Except for Amos Tutuola of "Palmwine Drinkard" fame, writers in this part of Africa are university graduates. They and other graduates can now look back on their past and on the strands of continuity in the culture of their communities with-

* He has since changed his name to Kofi Awoonor.

out a sense of shame. They are now keen to collect the oral literature of their societies for research purposes, to try to locate the point where the rupture set in, and to see what use they can make of the literature. Oral forms will certainly be of greater interest to those who want to write in their vernacular languages. An African writer will argue that he chooses to write in English so as to reach a wider reading public; and he will say that in his formative years he was too busy learning to master the tools that gave the colonial overlord power to give attention to his own vernacular as a literary medium. Literacy in English was one of these tools. But as English is only a political medium of communication—spoken only by the educated for inter-tribal understanding and not by the masses—there is not the setting to nourish the writer's language as there is for writers who are surrounded by people who speak English all the time. He finds that for the sake of authenticity he has to continue to listen to the speech idiom of his people and try to put across his thoughts in English without fear of sounding un-English.

East African writing shows the same trend as that in West Africa. The problems are mostly similar. The exception is that Swahili is a very close competitor of English as a literary language, in a way West African languages are not. It has evolved a rich vocabulary and idiom and has an old poetic tradition. Novelists still have to emerge who will use Swahili. Meantime there are those who write in English, like Kenya's novelists James Ngugi and Grace Ogot and others, who are publishing short stories and political and social comment. There is the same general theme running through their work as in West African writing—the relation between the new and the old. In addition, there has been the ten-year-long state of emergency and the Mau Mau phenomenon; one does not begin to feel the degree to which these ten years shook Kenyans until one reads their stories.

Africans in this region have not yet been given the opportunity to decide whether they want to be fully committed to urban life or not. A self-contained urban culture has to be given time to evolve. Already an exciting popular guitar music is flourishing. East Africans who, like South Africans, have a marked sense of melody and harmony, have put the guitar to vital popular use in a way West Africans have done with percussion instruments.

Outside the Kamba carvings, which have now become slick souvenir craftwork for the tourist industry, there are very interesting carvings of a complex surrealist form produced by the Makonde of South Tanganyika.* Carving as an art is not so widespread here as in West Africa. There are also several painters with remarkable ability. As they have little to refer to in the form of a three-dimensional traditional idiom, such as the West African wood carvings, the painters have to rely entirely on the crafts and the verbal arts of their people. This is in itself very rich material. They also reflect in their work the shock that accompanies a confrontation with a foreign culture. Because so many graduates from the fine-arts departments of the colleges are absorbed into the teaching profession, there have emerged less than a handful of full-time painters and sculptors in this region in the last twenty-eight years during which the fine arts have been taught at Makerere College in Uganda. Those who are coming out now are becoming conscious of the heavy missionary influence in their art and want to do something about it. If the dialogue about the "African Personality"—however uncritical it may be—achieves nothing else, it will have at least shaken these artists out of their complacency and created a climate in which the purely representational idiom that abounds at present will take on the dimension of social criticism or social significance.

Writing and painting in South Africa, as can be imagined, give expression to the physical and mental agony experienced in a life I have intimated earlier. There is plenty of protest, rejection of the status quo; there are also romantic-escapist moods, and somewhere rejection meets acceptance. There is sensuous imagery, and the writer and the artist record minute-by-minute experience, quivering with an impressionism that they have assimilated from American Negro jazz and literature.

*** The country has since changed its name to Tanzania.**

These artists, like their communities, take their African-ness for granted and merely assert their human dignity; the African in them is there, resisting and yielding in turn to the pressures of town life and European values. Fiction writers like Richard Rive, Alex la Guma, Can Themba, Casey Motsisi, Arthur Maimane, Peter Abrahams, and others take their cue mainly from the American Negro tradition.

There are several vernacular writers. Sotho, Xhosa, and Zulu have been literary media for nearly a century now. Much of the oral literature has also been recorded over the forty years that Bantu languages have been the subject of university study and research in South Africa. There are Bantu novels with adult ideas as distinct from the volume of small "readers" that are being published for schoolchildren in and outside South Africa. Some of these novels have become classics. It is significant that Bantu literature in South Africa engages itself with the theme of alienation as a result of the impact of European culture on the indigenous—a subject that does not worry the writer who uses English; the latter falls in the urban stream of consciousness in which people are sure not only that they want to be city dwellers but also what kind they want to be.

III

There are Africans who, prompted by their vision of a culturally united Africa, feel that a Pan-African approach to the promotion of culture is more important than a national one. These are Negroes of French influence. In order that these assimilated men should search for the roots of African culture, their poetry, like that of Sédar Senghor, Birago, and David Diop, recalls the world of ancestral spirits, masks, shrines, sacrifices and smoking blood, naked feet dancing, and so on.

But it is only the elite who have been assimilated and who assert this importance of being Negro—*négritude*. The masses are naturally unaffected, and there is the same basic continuity in their lives that we see in most of black Africa. Again, the symbols of African culture recalled by *négritude*-inspired poetry are really the outward visible features; their essence or substance eludes the poet and French rhetoric does not make the search for it easier.

One only begins to understand the humiliation that the assimilated African feels, and his revulsion and anger against the European way of life, when one sees the extent to which the *centre culturel français* has entrenched itself as an institution in the former French colonies, resisting any non-French influence. Africans here are still very much dependent on institutions of higher education in France, and the African students there do not take *négritude* seriously. Dakar University is still as French as ever, while the universities in Ghana, Nigeria, and East Africa are now independent of London.

It may not be amiss to quote an excerpt from a talk I gave at a conference in Dakar on African literature in April, 1963:

> Who is so stupid as to deny the historical fact of *négritude* as both a protest and a positive assertion of African cultural values? All this is valid. What I do not accept is the way in which too much of the poetry inspired by it romanticizes Africa—as a symbol of innocence, purity, and artless primitiveness. I feel insulted when some people imply that Africa is not also a violent continent. I am a violent person, and proud of it because it is often a healthy human state of mind; some day I'm going to plunder, rape, set things on fire; I'm going to cut someone's throat; I'm going to subvert a government; I'm going to organize a *coup d'état;* yes, I'm going to oppress my own people; I'm going to hunt down the rich fat black men who bully the small, weak black men and destroy them; I'm going to become a capitalist, and woe to all who cross my path or who want to be my servants or chauffeurs and so on; I'm going to lead a breakaway church—there is money in it; I'm going to attack the black bourgeoisie while I cultivate a garden, rear dogs and parrots, listen to jazz and classics, read "culture," and so on. Yes, I'm also going to organize a strike. Don't you know that sometimes I kill to the rhythm of drums and cut the sinews of a baby to cure it of paralysis? . . .
>
> This is only a dramatization of what Africa can do and is doing. The image of Africa consists of all these and others. And *négritude* poetry pretends that they do not constitute the image and

leaves them out. So we are told only half—often even a falsified half—of the story of Africa. Sheer romanticism that fails to see the large landscape of the personality of the African makes bad poetry. Facile protest also makes bad poetry. The omission of these elements of a continent in turmoil reflects a defective poetic vision. The greatest poetry of Léopold Sédar Senghor is that which portrays in himself the meeting point of Europe and Africa. This is the most realistic and honest and most meaningful symbol of Africa—an ambivalent continent searching for equilibrium. This synthesis of Europe and Africa does not necessarily reject the Negroness of the African. An image of Africa that only glorifies our ancestors and celebrates our "purity" and "innocence" is an image of a continent lying in state.

Camara Laye's "Le Regard du roi," Ferdinand Oyono's "Le Vieux Nègre et la medaille," and Mongo Beti's "Le Pauvre Christ de Bomba" are not bullied by *négritude*. They are concerned with portraying the black-white encounter, and they do this, notwithstanding, with a devastating poetic sense of irony unmatched by any that one sees in the English novel by Africans. Nor does the fascinating work of the Congolese poet Tchikaya U'Tamsi require *négritude* to attain the power it has.

Négritude, while a valuable slogan politically, can, because its apostles have set it up as a principle of art, amount to self-enslavement—"autocolonization," to quote a French writer speaking of African politics and economics. We should not allow ourselves to be bullied at gunpoint into producing literature that is supposed to contain a *négritude* theme and style. For now we are told, also, that there is *un style négro-africain* and that therefore we have to sloganize and write to a march. We are also told that *négritude* is less a matter of theme than style.

I say, then, that *négritude* can go on as a sociopolitical slogan, but that it has no right to set itself up as a standard of literary performance; there I refuse to go along. I refuse to be put in a Negro file—for sociologists to come and examine me. And yet I am no less committed to the African revolution. Art unifies even while it distinguishes men; and I regard it as an insult to the African for anyone to suggest—as the apostles of *négritude* often do—that because we write independently on different themes in divers modes and styles all over Africa, we are therefore ripe victims of Balkanization.

Let *négritude* make the theme of literature if people want to use it. But we must remember that literature springs from an individual's experience in the context of the culture and assumptions of the group. In its effort to take in the whole man, literature also tries to see far ahead, to project a prophetic vision, such as a writer is capable of, based on contemporary experience. It must at least set in motion vibrations in us that will continue even after we have read it, prompting us to continue inquiring into its meaning. And literature and art are too big for *négritude;* this had better be left as a historical phase.

If African culture is worth anything at all, it should not require myths to prop it up. These thoughts are not new at all. I have come to them after physical and mental agony. And this is of course not my monopoly either. It is the price Africa has to pay. And if you thought that the end of colonialism was the end of the agony, then it is time to wake up.[2]

IV

A Pan African view of culture cannot be a substitute for the practical involvement, at different levels, of communities in national culture. It can and must reinforce national cultures. Ghana is perhaps the only African country where the government takes direct responsibility for organizing culture for everybody who cares for it. Through its Institute of Art and Culture the government channels money to regional cultural centers, and traditional music and theater inspired by traditional forms thrive for the enjoyment of all. The school of music and drama attached to the Institute of African Studies at the University of Ghana engages in research into oral literature, indigenous music and drama; students are surrounded with these forms even while they learn Western techniques. Somewhere they must find a point of integration. It is also admirable that Ghanaians should, through direct government responsibility, keep reminding themselves that culture is not something to dress up for, for

2. "Remarks on Négritude," by Ezekiel Mphahlele. From Ezekiel Mphahlele (ed.): *African Writing Today.* Copyright Ezekiel Mphahlele, 1967, pp. 247–252. Reprinted by permission of Penguin Books Ltd.

the elite, but to be lived by the maximum number of people; this the government makes possible.*

In the larger and the poorer countries, there is ample scope for private cultural institutions. In Nigeria, for instance, there are writers' and artists' clubs called Mbari—one each at Ibadan, Oshogbo, and Enugu. They promote music, theater, art, and creative writing with an African basis. The University of Ibadan's school of drama has gone into the creation of indigenous theater on a big scale. The school is also helping a popular Yoruba singing troupe in its programs, most impressive of which has been the recent adaptation of Amos Tutuola's "Palmwine Drinkard" for the stage, performed in Yoruba with music and dance.

There is a center in Nairobi similar to the Mbari and serving a similar function. It has the added role of harmonizing and reconciling tribal idioms and modes in music and dance toward the establishment of a national culture in Kenya. The Tanganyika† Government has a Ministry of National Culture and Youth. Unlike Ghana, this ministry organizes mostly national festivals and individual talent is not yet provided for. South Africa's Union Artists, with its Music and Drama Association, promotes musical shows such as the recent *King Kong* and *Sponono,* which have also been taken overseas. Individual music troupes are also being assisted by the Union. Here again, the accent is on African themes adapted to modern forms.

These institutions clearly point to the fact that there are groups of people who are concerned to strike a course that will lead them to a definition of the national culture within which they operate, who are concerned to bridge the gap between urban and rural cultures as a way of restoring equilibrium in fast-changing times. And it is perhaps the Western elements of these cultures that will yet be the unifying force as a common medium. The alternative to these national institutions, if we lose a sense of proportion, is for us to arrange huge Pan-African

* It should be noted that these activities took place under the government of Kuame Nkrumah.

† Tanzania.

get-togethers simply to glory in our corporate blackness, rail against some ill-defined neo-colonialism, talk culture in English and French, go back home and watch our traditional dances as something outside of ourselves, like tourists, without any inclination to live our cultures. One can foresee that our cultures are going to be exposed to more European influences and absorb more. There are other conditioning factors in our cultural development: the seemingly inevitable drive toward one-party states; toward African socialism with the family as the vital unit and pivot of what President Nyerere calls *ujamaa*—neighborliness; the establishment of departments of African studies in our universities. One thing is certain, if nothing else is: it is that the African wants to determine his cultural organization himself. And in many areas he wants to decolonize his mind.

Implications of Color Identity in Pan-Africanism

To look at the aggressive culture of the West and its impact on the passive cultures of Africa and the Orient, to look at Africans closing their ranks to assert their own "personality" as a defense against an alien white culture, urges one to speculate on the question: What would the African's attitude have been toward Western culture if the white people had never colonized Africa? Substitute "enslaved" for "colonized," and you add another dimension to the question. For when it comes to color groupings, the wildest and most agonizing generalizations can be made to justify such group attitudes and identify. And this is a two-way reaction between the poles of blackness and whiteness.

Western culture only followed after the harbingers of Western civilization had carved out routes for it: the explorers, the traders, the missionaries, prepared the way, consciously or not. Where African religions were passive, Christianity came out to proselytize. Where our way of life generally centered on the mere urge to be, Western civilization was by its very nature self-perpetuating and had to explore diverse ways of releasing itself. Where Western civilization grappled mostly with things, our way of life put a premium on human relations. Our religions centered on ancestral spirits and the worship of them on a family rather than an organized community basis such as we see in the Christian churchgoing practice. From all this, it is reasonable to conclude that Western civilization and culture would, by their very nature, still have released their aggressive energy and made inroads into Africa. It is reasonable to assume, too, that, because of the methods of attack this civilization uses —high-powered advertising, rapid communications, including literature, mass media—it is inherently a colonizing civilization. It seems obvious that even if political, military, and economic imperialism had not broken upon us, we should have found ourselves in some condition of colonization.

What would our color attitudes have been, then, as distinct from those we see emerging among ourselves from a condition of political subjugation and slavery? Quite clearly, the basic ascendency-submission, superior-inferior, and master-servant relationships would have arisen because of what we have said about the aggressiveness of white civilization. But maybe we should have had a fighting chance to be able to direct and control the change that came upon us. For inasmuch as a proselytizing alien religion and culture came to passive peoples, riding on breathtaking machines and captivating neon lights, and found them unorganized as nations, we now realize what a built-in capacity for change we have as Negro Africans. It is a capacity one does not see at all among, say, Indians.

What also made it easy for Christianity and Islam and the trappings of white civilization to entrench themselves where they did in Africa was the fact of human relationships as the very center of our tribal cultures. In times of peace, or in cases where you did not suspect witchcraft as the motive of a visit, you took a guest, no matter where he came from, as he was, and treated him as a human being. Nor did it matter if he came from what your people regarded as an inferior clan. Because of this, we have often been taken in by missionaries, traders, explorers, administrators from abroad. Historical colonialism, therefore, pointed up sharply, and even became the *raison d'être* of, the clash of color. A hypothetical situation of independence such as we have referred to above, in which the African would, from a point of strength and human dignity that flourish in political self-determination, defend his way of life, might even have contained color conflicts better.

As it is, we now have to clean up the mess. At the negotiating table where white and black must bargain, the black man has the deep-seated suspicion that the white man will, as he has always been prone to do throughout the history of his encounter with blacks, try to deal the cards fraudulently. We now want to scrap the textbooks we have been fed on while the white man directed our education—textbooks that glorify whiteness, white courage, white ingenuity, and even the white man's ability to rule others. Even those who have not really suffered the humiliation, the brutality, and the violence that the southern African Negroes are experiencing at the hands of white people feel a compulsion to sniff around for neo-colonialism, real or imaginary. Students who had no critical judgment at all about their British-oriented primary and secondary schooling attain university level when the colonial master has left. Fascism in non-independent parts of Africa generates a kind of indignation in them which can only be an intellectual projection. And, of course, color does not need to be physically and actively present to be able to whip up violent emotions, even though its presence intensifies them. This is some of the mess we are left with in independent African countries.

When *négritude* was first conceived in the 1930's by Aimé Césaire, the Martinique Negro poet who was then studying in Paris, it referred simply to the general character of the Negro's artistic expression and its themes about the Negro's past and present condition. As a social concept, it aimed at restoring the Negro's confidence in himself as a black man; it was to restore in him a pride in his African ancestry. The content of the poetry composed within this frame of reference and inspired by the sense of pride it generated, highlighted such external features of African humanism as were immediately available to the writer, making them an organic part of a beautiful myth-making lyricism.

On *négritude,* for example, Césaire says, "It dives into the flowing flesh of the sky/Piercing the weight of oppression with its erect patience." In his poem "Africa," he says:

a wound of today is a womb of the orient
a shuddering which rises from the black forgotten fires,
it is
the ruin risen from the ash, bitter word of scars
all lithe and new, a visage
of old, bird of scorn, bird reborn, brother of the sun.[1]

This was really a development of a theme begun by Caribbean poets in the late 1920's. Haiti's Jacques Roumain sees Guinea as a Negro heaven: "a smoky sky pierced by the cry of birds"; "There, there awaits you beside the water a quiet village/ And the hut of your fathers, and the hard ancestral stone where your head will rest at last." [2] Cuba's Nicolás Guillén writes:

Have I got an ancestor of night
with a large black mark
(blacker than the skin)
a large mark
written with a whip? [3]

Much later, French Guiana's Léon Damas wrote in his "Pigments":

Do they really dare to treat me as white
while I aspire to be nothing but Negro
and while they are looting my Africa:[4]

On the eve of World War II, Césaire had this to say in his *Cahier d'un retour au pays natal*:

1. From Gerald Moore, *Seven African Writers* (London: Oxford University Press, 1962), p. x.
2. From *An Anthology of Contemporary Latin American Poetry*, edited by Dudley Fitts. Copyright 1942 by New Directions Publishing Corporation. Reprinted by permission of New Directions Publishing Corporation.
3. From Gerald Moore, *Seven African Writers* (London: Oxford University Press, 1962), p. xii.
4. From Léon Damas, *Black-Label* (Paris: Editions Gallimard, 1956). © Editions Gallimard 1956. Reprinted by permission of the publisher.

Listen to the white world
How their defeats sound in their victories[5]

This assertion of the importance of being black is, then, originally Caribbean and Afro-American. Negro writers like Jamaica-born Claude McKay, America's Langston Hughes and Countee Cullen, also gave at times lyrical and at times prosaic expression of the idea of blackness. But just as there were whites in Haiti who glorified "primitive innocent Africa," there were white Americans like Carl Van Vechten who admired these Negro poets. In his *Nigger Heaven,*[6] he portrays Harlem night spots as places which recall the passions, the pagan rhythms, and lust for life commonly associated with "primitive Africa."

These Caribbeans and Afro-Americans felt the situation of exile and the need for identity with Africa much more keenly and deeply than African *négritude* poets did who followed the lead, on their front, of Léopold Sédar Senghor.

Not only did the African French poets merely idealize the outward trappings of African traditional life, the inner essence of which they could never grasp or penetrate owing to their alienation, but also their poetry was a dialogue among only the elite. The folk in the African hinterland continued to live their indigenous tribal cultures, pure or evolved.

Color sensibilities, then, are sharp among the elite in Africa, since they began to express themselves as a defensive measure—as a response to an attack from across the color line. And the tools of expression were first acquired by the elite through education, which also provides the content and idiom of protest by the awareness and discontent it sparks off.

The "African Personality," which is usually regarded as a political manifestation of the same assertion of African values of which *négritude* is a poetic expression, should really just mean the aggregate of cultural traits that are common to Africa: a common pool of such tribal ways of life that can be

5. These two lines are taken from *Cahier d'un retour au pays natal* (*Return to My Native Land*) by Aimé Césaire, published by *Présence Africaine,* Paris (1956).

6. Carl Van Vechten, *Nigger Heaven* (New York: Alfred A. Knopf, 1926).

said to make up an African way of life, an African consciousness, roughly south of the Sahara. These are, for instance, communal responsibility born of the African tendency for the individual to lean on the group for approval, censure, and general moral support; the reverence for ancestral spirits; respect for one's elders; generally relaxed sex attitudes that are free of the neuroses and complexes one observes in Christian-Western sex relationships; love of life as an end in itself. As our politicians use the phrase on the public platform, "African Personality" may merely mean *la présence africaine* in world affairs; or simply the African's newly acquired right of self-determination. When they try to come closer to its cultural implications, they merely succeed in indicating African traditions as a collection of museum pieces in a glass cage: which is why they often exhort their listeners to "preserve" African traditions, never conceiving these as part of a living culture and therefore subject to the checks and balances, profit and loss involved in the processes of culture change.

At their worst, *négritude* and the African Personality take up a color attitude, such as Senghor adopts (which his best poetry refutes), and such as can be seen in Léon Damas's stance when he says that beauty, wisdom, endurance, courage, patience, charm, love, rhythm, art, laughter, joy, peace are Negro. At its best, *négritude,* as a social concept, marked a historical phase that should have helped the elite to seek and find anchor in the positive values of their people. At its best, the African Personality is, in Mr. Alex Quaison-Sackey's words: "in the largest sense the cultural expression of what is common to all peoples whose home is on the continent of Africa." [7] This refers to something positive in it, and it has no color connotations. As Mr. W. E. Abraham, the Ghanaian philosopher, says: "When one speaks of the unity of African cultures, one does not necessarily wish to say that there is a certain minimal complex of significant elements which are common to African cultures and which

7. Alex Quaison-Sackey, *Africa Unbound* (New York: Praeger, 1963), p. 36. Reprinted by permission of Praeger Publishers and Andre Deutsch Limited.

are such that they have never been seen elsewhere before in the history of mankind." [8] Here again, there is no color stance. It is interesting to notice, though, that in a moment of something like incorrigible but sincere idealism, Mr. Quaison-Sackey comes quite close to this sense of uniqueness. And here we are rocketed into the realm of speculation, which he himself acknowledges:

> The African Personality—by attempting to transcend its specific physical and intellectual environment, yet without pulling up the roots that nourish it—hopes to create, as a force for world peace and unity, a dynamic political creed. Such a creed will express itself through that personality which embraces the qualities of man both as citizen of Africa and as a member of the human race. In other words, the African Personality is extremely active and vital; it is, in fact, an ideal; and like any ideal, it is difficult both to define and to realize for it is subject to various interpretations.[9]

Color exclusiveness cannot be ruled out as one of these interpretations, either within or outside the group. One is inclined to ask what it is that is distinctively African which our continent can contribute to world peace.

Négritude and the African Personality can be said to be the cultural flank of Pan-Africanism. They are recent arrivals in this role, and they have brought to latter-day Pan-Africanism an element of exclusiveness based on color identity. Between 1900, when the first Pan-African Congress was held in London, through three subsequent ones and the fifth congress in 1945, Pan-Africanism was based on a general sense of belonging in a color camp. This made it possible for men outside Africa, like the American Negro Dr. W. E. B. Du Bois, who set the pace for the 1900 congress, and the West Indians Dr. H. Sylvester Williams and George Padmore, to come under the banner.

However, Dr. Edward D. Blyden's presidential address of 1881 at Liberia College, Monrovia, has also some relevance here, as the audience he was exhorting consisted of Negroes who

8. W. E. Abraham, *The Mind of Africa* (London: George Weidenfeld & Nicolson, 1962), p. 115. Reprinted by permission of the publisher.

9. Quaison-Sackey, *Africa Unbound,* p. 37.

had been uprooted by slavery and returned to Africa. Cultural identity implied here is based on a common desire to recapture African roots:

> We must not suppose that the Anglo-Saxon methods are final, that there is nothing for us to find out for our own guidance, and that we have nothing to teach to the world. There is inspiration for us also. We must study our brethren in the interior (the indigènes) who know better than we do the laws of growth for the race. . . . We look too much to foreigners and are dazzled almost to blindness by the exploits, so as to fancy that they have exhausted the possibilities of humanity.[10]

The same noble sentiments were later to form the basis of the *négritude* impulse among the African students in Paris. Dr. Blyden goes on to say:

> The true principle of mental culture is perhaps this: to preserve an accurate balance between the studies which carry the mind out of itself, and those which recall it home again. When we receive impressions from without we must bring from our own consciousness the idea that gives them shape; we must mould them by our own individuality. Now, in looking over the whole world I see no place where this sort of culture for the Negro can be better secured than in Africa; where he may, with less interruptions from surrounding influences, find out his place and his work, develop his peculiar gifts and powers; and for the training of Negro youth upon the basis of their own idiosyncrasies, with a sense of race individuality, self-respect, and liberty.[10]

After 1945, there was a lull in Pan-African affairs. Political struggles in Africa were being localized and nationalism was growing apace. One would have expected that nationalism would point up sharply a keen color consciousness aimed not simply at colonialism generally, but at individual white people. Yet, in addition to the fact that foreign rule in British and French colonies south of the Sahara did not release nearly half as much mental and physical agony and racial tension as in

10. Quoted by Colin Legum in *Pan-Africanism* (New York: Praeger, 1962), p. 264. Reprinted by permission of Praeger Publishers and Pall Mall Press Ltd.

South Africa and Algeria and, lately, as in Mozambique and Angola, the British and the French retreated gracefully, Belgium in disorder, in the face of advancing black nationalism. Generally, color friction had no bottom—no basis in physical proximity and the resultant politics of integration, segregation, and competition between large numbers of blacks and whites as we have in North America and South Africa. Nationalism has up till now merely been inspired by an urge for self-determination.

There have been earlier forms of African nationalism that had, in correspondence to Pan-Africanism in its earlier and more inclusive stages, a very strong element of color identity. The wars between the Africans and the Boer intruders in South Africa from about the middle of the eighteenth to the middle of the nineteenth centuries were characterized by mutual color-ridden hatred. The white man, not just the foreign ruler or intruder, was to be driven into the sea. The last would-be full-scale revolt to be organized against whites in South Africa was the Bambata Rebellion of 1906. Some historians have related the Prester John legend to this rebellion, in which the leader is both a political and spiritual figure. Prester John was to vindicate the black man's religion—a mixture of Christianity and black magic. In later years, Negro political leaders in South Africa were to try to negotiate with their white rulers, taking literally their loudly proclaimed Christian ethics. They were to try to extract concessions from the white man or fight him on the latter's own terms, i.e., by constitutional means. The glitter of Western education as well as its power blunted the edge of anti-white bitterness as a color phenomenon. And now, since the white man has begun to undermine legalistic humanistic, and even his own professed Christian ethics, and since he has broken all bridges down, black and white have once again become extremely color-conscious and polarized.

The Prester John legend takes the mind on to Ethiopianism, a form of black nationalism that was inspired by the desire for religious independence. Ethiopianism, Messrs. George Shepperson and Thomas Price explain in their book *Independent*

African, took its etymological origins from the Bible, e.g., "Ethiopia shall soon stretch out her hands to God" (Psalm 68:31). Its political character, they observe, may have been inspired by the Abyssinian defeat of the Italians at Adowa in 1896.

> But for the most of the last three decades of the nineteenth century and for the first two of the twentieth, it was to stand for a form of religious African nationalism which always threatened to boil over into revolt against European rule. Ethiopianism had its origins in South Africa in the 1870's when prejudice had stung many Africans to set up their own churches rather than face segregation and humiliation in the white man's place of worship.[11]

The authors point out that the people who felt humiliation most acutely were the ministers and leading members, such as deacons of the Christian churches that had been established by white missionaries. A class of African ministers who had fought their way up through such education as was available to them, spoke politics in the language of the Bible. The movement came to strike terror into the hearts of whites who must have conjured in their own minds pictures of gruesome slaughter by blacks. This would vindicate their stock view that "civilization" could never go deep in black folk.

John Chilembwe of Nyasaland, who was sent to the United States by American Negro Baptists for his education, caught the fever of Ethiopianism and was later to lead the "Nyasaland Native Rising" of 1915 against the whites.

The first separatist tribal church, as a breakaway from an established white church, was formed in 1884 by an African Wesleyan minister in Tembuland, Cape Province: this started off the Ethiopian movement proper. In 1892, another African Wesleyan preacher established a general "Ethiopian" church. It sought and obtained affiliation to the African Methodist Episcopal Church (A.M.E.), an independent Negro institution in the

11. George Shepperson and Thomas Price, *Independent African: John Chilembwe and the Origins, Setting and Significance of the Nyasaland Native Rising of 1915* (Edinburgh: Edinburgh University Press, 1958), p. 72. Reprinted by permission of the publisher.

United States. Up till this day, this church is always referred to in South African Bantu languages as the church of "Topia" (Church of Ethiopia). To create the climate for this affiliation, the United States A.M.E. sent its Bishop, Henry M. Turner, to tour South African independent churches. Turner's idea that it was the "manifest destiny of colored Americans to redeem their unhappy brethren in Africa" [12] affected the Africans themselves. American Negroes thus had tremendous influence in South Africa in the mid-1890's. Their presence and attachment to the South African independent churches accentuated the color theme in the drama of religious separatism. The political significance of the American schools and colleges which Negroes and Africans attended did not escape the whites in southern and central Africa, and they became restless.

The back-to-Africa call of the American Negro Marcus Garvey in the early 1920's rang across to Africa and sent a ripple of enthusiasm and hope through the promoters of Ethiopianism, at any rate while Garvey lasted.

An American Negro Baptist minister is quoted as having said:

> If it be here shown beyond reasonable doubt . . . that the ancient Egyptians, Ethiopians, and Libyans . . . were the ancestors of the present race of Ham, then the Negro of the nineteenth century may point to them with pride; and with all who would find in him a man and a brother, cherish the hope of a return to racial celebrity, when in the light of a Christian civilization, Ethiopia shall stretch out her hands unto God.[13]

Like political nationalism, Ethiopianism diminished in importance as an anti-white phenomenon. But, unlike the general revival of anti-white suspicion and in parts even hatred of whites in political activity recently, Ethiopianism never regained its color aspect. More churches have broken away to become independent since 1884, but they have tended to become progressively apolitical and an expression of social frustration and personality feuds. As they have now to be registered by the

12. *Ibid.,* p. 73.
13. *Ibid.,* p. 102.

government, they have to follow the dictates of apartheid in order to survive.

Outside southern Africa, one finds a tremendous fund of tolerance on the part of Africans toward whites. In a situation of political independence, self-confidence and a relative sense of security are bound to grow among the indigenous peoples; "relative" because they still need foreign technical and professional assistance. In such conditions, "Africanization" of jobs can often cause tension between racial groups. But by and large when people can speak from a position of political strength, economic interindependence does not bring about the humiliation economic dependence can breed. But the former has also the positive effect of creating an area of intercourse between black and white.

Then there is the world intellectual community which Africans have entered. Education helps reconcile the very conflicts, fears, and areas of discontentment and yearning it sets up in the individual. We assimilate Western education until we make it ours. There comes a point at which African and Western concerns coincide. This is particularly so with regard to relationships between the educated and less educated or illiterate, between the urban and rural streams of consciousness. Education throws you out of your community and boosts and promotes individual talent. This goes against the African's traditional sense of community. The deficiencies of a colonial education in relation to African needs have merely been superimposed upon what is a universal problem—the alienation of the individual. The nostalgia the African elite evince for their African traditions has a parallel in the yearning the Western elite show for the simplicity, frankness, and realness of working-class life. There has come about a rupture between culture and technological civilization in highly developed societies, and also a rupture between religion and high culture. In African communities, religion was an organic part of culture, and culture a functional aid in the growing-up process in the individual. It does not seem as if we are going to escape involvement in the concern of Western man over the atomization of his way of life. Already it is happening in Africa, and in the face of this common anxiety, color becomes irrelevant. We all—black or white—have to master the external world and become integrated personalities. The color clash has greatly diminished within the intellectual community.

When the Pan-African movement was revived, it was on African soil. The first rallying together on new ground was the All-African People's Conference of December, 1958, in Accra, with a year-old independent state of Ghana taking the lead and setting the pace. Most of the countries were represented at the get-together by freedom fighters, as they were still under foreign rule. It was colonialism that brought the Africans together. Apart from subsequent conferences held where both independent states and representatives of freedom movements reasserted their solidarity without creating any machinery to realize Pan-African ideals, a lull once more followed. Now we have this machinery in the form of the Organization of African Unity (OAU).

Southern Africa is still in the turmoil of racial strife, and yet one does not observe in other parts of our continent anti-white feeling or a positive glorification of blackness such as we saw in earlier Pan-Africanism when the American and West Indian Negroes stood in the front line. Now, it is African independence that inspires American Negroes and gives them a new sense of pride as black people.

Apart from an expressed wish to help liberate the southern African underdog and the provision of a body like the Liberation Committee, the *raison d'être* of the OAU has something much more to do with the urgent need for Africa to unite in economic and political planning against disease, poverty, and ignorance than with the preservation of a color identity.

Group attitudes present a posture of solidarity, of unity of thinking. Particularly within as broad a framework as that of Pan-Africanism, they often falsify the ambivalence of the individual. Black and white individuals meet and react to each other. It is difficult to imagine that a white man can come to Africa, even as a mere cold-bloodedly detached administrator, stay for two or more years, and leave us without his color attitudes having been hardened or softened or challenged in one way or another. The same thing must happen to a hard-core African nationalist who lives in Europe for two years or more. In the most brutal situation, such as the South African one, attachments between black and white can be surprisingly warm and lasting at the individual level, even more so than in African countries where whites are not entrenched.

When different races have lived together as long as they have in South Africa, it is easy to imagine that, even in their segregated existence, the non-whites should master the techniques of handling the various shifts, dodges, and conflicts of the encounter. And there is a sense in which the African, who has fashioned a robust and self-sufficient urban culture, feels he is on top of things. *He* has always been the one to give an account of himself to the white boss. *He* has always been the one to reject this and accept that over three countries. In many ways he feels superior to the white man who, by virtue of his color, is absolved from the responsibility of manipulating the encounter and thereby learning something. At the same time one foresees a violent and savage clash between black and white, the immediate results of which must fortify the sense of color identity. Mr. Nelson Mandela, the South African political leader and prisoner now serving a life sentence on Robben Island, declared during his trial that nationalism was for the Negroes of South Africa a concept of freedom and fulfillment in their own land. He has been tried in the fire as a leader, and the people arrived at this point through physical and mental agony.

And so the paradoxes and ironies continue to be acted out in Africa and in the Negro world at large. The culturally self-sufficient West African who has been through a British-type education has a frank admiration for things European, including institutions of learning, even while he may despise American and West Indian Negroes. The French-speaking intellectual often feels superior to *les Africains anglophones* in a measure that corresponds to the high esteem the French have for their own culture. Sometimes they let loose about the moral deficiencies of Europe in defense of *négritude* while they continue to live in Paris and take part in French culture. The culturally inadequate elite of East Africa, who are comparative newcomers in their class, naturally still have much confidence in white culture and are often even unaware of their own immense capabilities.

All these paradoxes which are acted out between individuals make it impossible for us to assess satisfactorily the assertion of color either within or outside the Pan-African movement. We do know that the sense of cultural distinctiveness can become a powerful factor.

Much has been made of the increasing importance of the voice of colored peoples in world organizations like the United Nations. It is difficult to assess this in terms of an increasing sense of color identity among the darker-skinned communities of the world. And yet the pockets of color conflicts that still remain in the world are violent enough to cast a shadow of foreboding over the prospect of world citizenship. Will the world find itself in this half of the twentieth century divided into two color camps? This could be, if the Afro-Asian bloc felt more and more committed to defend Negroes against white barbarism. The operative word here is "defend." And yet one keeps wondering if we have any right to think that "Afro-Asian" implies the unity of dark-skinned peoples. Arabs, Indians, and Chinese have displayed shocking arrogance toward Africans for as long as we have known them.

African Writers and Commitment

If you set out deliberately to make one-sided statements to a mass audience in order to advocate a point of view, then you are making propaganda. This should be distinguished from such closely allied uses of communication as instruction, information, and inquiry. You are advocating something if you select material from some channel of communication which is meant to influence attitudes on controversial issues. When the government distributes a pamphlet on what to do to help combat illiteracy, the act is instructive, it is not propaganda, unless the need for mass literacy is in question. It is inquiry, not propaganda, to analyze controversial doctrines like capitalism or communism for the sake of enlightening others.

What we hear and what we see make the most effective media of propaganda. You see a drawing or a painting or a poster that shows the ravages of a disease or the agony of forced labor, or a rioter holding a firebrand and shouting: "Burn baby, burn!," or you hear a speaker urge you to go on strike. You feel that the message in either case comes direct and registers in quick time. Drama combines both the visual and the oral. It is conceived in terms of presentation on the stage. It is accordingly a most effective weapon in educating for an immediate end.

George Bernard Shaw, John Galsworthy, Brecht, Jean-Paul Sartre, Ibsen, Chekhov, and then the crop of angry playwrights of the late 1950's and the early part of this decade like John

---

This essay was originally printed as "Writers and Commitment" in *Black Orpheus,* II, No. 3 (1968), pp. 34–39.

Osborne, Arnold Wesker, Wole Soyinka, and so on—all these were concerned with the predicament of man in a hostile environment and with the sickness that we all see in highly developed societies. They dramatize this predicament, showing us in the process a portion of life on the stage.

Are they propagating a doctrine or belief, or advocating a point of view? To a very large extent they are doing this, but in different ways. Some, like Shaw, tell us more or less what they stand for in long prefaces so that we understand more fully what they mean in their dramatic presentations. Others are more subtle, but the message registers. It may be the irrelevance or death of aristocracy as Chekhov represents; or the woman's assertion of her independence as in Ibsen; or the courage of woman as in Brecht; or it may be a portrayal of the working class as a community that feels life at its most basic and real levels, as in the kitchen-sink playwrights; or the loneliness of the intellectual; or the futility and cruelty of class or religious snobbery; or the loneliness of the political prisoner as in Wole Soyinka; or the brutality of American race attitudes as in Lorraine Hansberry and James Baldwin.

Perhaps it is a measure of a dramatist's success as an artist when he can move us and pleasurably teach us without any offensive propaganda, precisely because this is a medium which lends itself easiest to the propagating of ideas. For at his most naïve, he merely needs an explosive situation to represent and then simply to talk through his characters. Yet, for reasons I cannot pretend to understand, blatant propaganda in itself seldom if ever offends when served up from a theater stage, while it offends easily in fiction and verse, is boring or embarrassing.

Propaganda is always going to be with us. There will always be the passionate outcry against injustice, war, fascism, poverty. It will keep coming at us, reminding us that man is as wicked as he is noble and that the mass audience out there is waiting to be stirred by passionate words. African literature, like the other literatures of the world, is never going to be totally free of propaganda. But to say this is not to say propaganda is necessarily conducive to great literature, no matter *how* it is served up. It was Brecht in "Kuenergeschichten" who put the following words in a character's mouth:

> I have noticed that we frighten many people away from our doctrines, because we appear to have an answer to everything. Should we not, in the interests of our propaganda, draw up a list of those problems that we consider totally unsolved? [1]

Indeed, in great literature propaganda cannot be easily separated from the world that is conceived by the author and the manner in which he presents it.

Before we talk specifically about African literature, let us look at various aspects of commitment as it prompts propaganda. Commitment need not give rise to propaganda: the writer can make his stand known without advocating it openly or in two-dimensional terms, i.e., in terms of one response to one stimulus. People tend to suspect political commitment. Yet politics are a human activity. In ancient Greece and in the Middle Ages there was not this dividing line between politics and other areas of human activity.

Every writer is committed to something beyond his art, to a statement of value not purely aesthetic, to a "criticism of life." Existentialist philosophers regard liberty as an integral feature of the human condition itself. Man is freedom. Jean-Paul Sartre, one of the leading French philosophers and writers, and himself an existentialist, insists that this view of liberty should be an important factor in literary criticism: "The writer, a free man addressing free men, has only one subject—freedom." [2]

The writer assumes a respect for human freedom even as he writes. But Sartre is not content with this as a mere attitude: it needs a political purpose. Literature must be made to serve a political purpose. For him literature, truth, democracy, and other human values are bound up in a kind of program. The question is—and the same question may well be posed in con-

1. Quoted by John Mander, *The Writer and Commitment* (London: Martin Secker and Warburg, 1961), p. 6. Reprinted by permission of the publisher.

2. Quoted in Mander, p. 9.

nection with that wing of Communist culture in Russia that insists on a social and political program for the writer and artist in general—whether the respect for freedom and mankind as the absolute entity toward which all things must move can always be contained by literature and its other concerns like structures, its forms, its styles? Can Sartre's kind of discipline and aims for literature become inviolable rules for a craft that is always breaking rules, breaking down myths?

Somehow Sartre's thoughts about commitment did not take root in England, even in the late 1940's when he was most prominent. Perhaps this was because most of Sartre's works were not yet translated into English; it may be that something native in the English intellect or creative spirit resisted Sartre's kind of discipline, and generally the French habit of interpreting literature in philosophical terms. Instead of his influence, we see the new Left growing out of new alliances and affiliations. This comprised Raymond Williams, Richard Hogart, John Osborne, Arnold Wesker, and so on. But its commitment was sociological: it was concerned with a new vision of society. It was not philosophical or literary. The writer on the other hand managed to contain in his craft a number of beliefs and ideologies that were opposed to one another even while he took a stand on the whole question of the national diffusion of culture, because he rejected the idea of culture as a privilege of the elite.

For some strange reason Sartre excluded poetry from his scheme of commitment. Poetry was "opaque," "non-communicative," while prose was "transparent," "communicative," and used words as means, as distinct from poetry that used words as an end. So prose was best suited as a tool for the committed writer. And commitment for the existentialist comes out of a sense of responsibility. To be committed means to be responsible.

Yet Sartre in his introduction, *Orphée Noire,* to Senghor's anthology of African and Malagasy poetry encourages by implication the *négritude* movement as anti-racist racism. He seems to recognize African poetry as a fit vehicle to propagate a creed. After Sartre, several people have claimed that African literature is "functional," meaning, I believe, that this writing advocates the black man's cause and/or instructs its audience. This claim indicates a dangerous tendency, which is to draw a line of distinction between a function in which an author vindicates or asserts black pride or takes a sociopolitical stand and a function in which he seeks to stir humanity as a whole. At any rate it is dangerous for literature, which even while it particularizes, literature takes in wider circles of humanity. The functions overlap, and the bigger the rift between them the more stridently its propaganda yells out, the more life's ironies and paradoxes are overlooked, and the more the reader feels his sense of belonging assailed or unduly exploited. It is not that protest is necessarily faulty: indeed all art that humanity identifies itself with is a kind of protest, a criticism of life. Much depends on the writer's vision and the way he protests.

All the same, in spite of Sartre's sanctions, Africans have found poetry more readily available as a weapon of propaganda, etc., than prose fiction or even the essay. The following example (from "The Blackman's God," [3] by Frank Kobina Parkes of Ghana) will show how badly propaganda has been handled:

Our God is great
Who dare deny it?
Our God is great
Powerful and dark
Peering through ages
Healing, killing, guiding along.

Our God is black
And like any goddamned god
Guiding when loving
Killing when angered.

Our God is like all gods
Slow to anger when fed fat on yams
And of great mercy when suckled on blood

3. Frank Kobina Parkes, *Songs from the Wilderness* (London: University of London Press, 1965), p. 16. Reprinted by permission of the publisher.

Brothers, blackmen, unbelievers
Our God is like all gods
Powerful and blood-loving.

In most of his poems, Parkes writes much, much better than this. This poem is only valid if Parkes is talking with his tongue in his cheek, or if he is saying, in effect, "If we *must* have a god, it doesn't matter which one he'll be—we've had it anyway." But if he is serious and is actually upholding the black man's traditional gods because they are "black," the verse crumbles as a propaganda piece. It purports to answer all the questions about God. It assumes the need for a God right away, and the poet pretends to know everything about the intentions of His moods—when and how He wants to punish and reward—all in the context of so much suffering in the world! If we are being told man is pathetically helpless under such a God, the statement is not worth making—we are none the wiser. Even before *négritude* or Negrismo was coined, W. E. B. Du Bois was singing:

I am the Smoke King
I am black.
I am darkening with song,
I am hearkening to wrong;
I will be black as blackness can
The blacker the mantle the mightier the man.[4]

Other American Negro poets hammered out the same theme to counteract their rejection by whites. *Négritude* caught on with the Caribbeans and then with the Africans. And now that colonialism has receded, even though its trappings remain, the Afro-Americans have taken it back as it were and are producing volumes of verse vindicating their black pride, using propaganda in a most sophisticated and often angry, incisive, and moving idiom. These Afro-American poets have mastered the

4. From John Henrik Clarke (ed.), "Selected Poems of W. E. B. Du Bois," *Freedomways*, V, No. 1 (Winter, 1965), 88. Reprinted by permission of Freedomways Associates.

language of "felt thought." They do not try to use rhetoric to do their feeling and thinking for them in the way so much of our African black pride verse does. The poignancy that we read in the American and Caribbean poetry of alienation shows again and again that this is where *négritude* began; that it was not mere gesturing but alienation that was felt deep down to the marrow; that so much of it in Africa was derivative and rode on a rhetoric that flew like flakes at a second reading.

There are some fine voices of propaganda to be heard in African poetry which either bring out the distilled essence of *négritude* because it is beyond mere gesturing, or expresses the agony of white oppression. Léopold Sédar Senghor can say in his "Prayer to Masks":

> For who else would teach rhythm to the world
> that has died of machines and cannons?
>
> For who else should ejaculate the cry of joy,
> that arouses the dead and the wise in a new dawn?
> Say, who else could return the memory of life
> to men with a torn hope?
>
> . . . .
>
> They call us men of death
> But we are the men of the dance whose feet
> only gain power when they beat the hard soil.[5]

Kofi Awoonor speaks of the moment of rediscovering ourselves:

> It cannot be the music we heard that night
> and still lingers in the chambers of memory
> It is the new chorus of our forgotten comrades
> and the halleluyas of our second selves.[6]

5. Translation by George Moore and Ulli Beier. From *Modern Poetry from Africa,* ed. George Moore and Ulli Beier. Copyright George Moore and Ulli Beier, 1963, p. 54. Reprinted by permission of Penguin Books Ltd.

6. "Rediscovery and Other Poems," in Ezekiel Mphahlele (ed.), *African Writing Today* (Harmondsworth: Penguin, 1967), p. 96. Reprinted by permission of Kofi Awoonor.

Gabriel Okara, on himself as the meeting point between two modes of life, piano and drums:

> And I lost in the morning mist
> of an age at a riverside keep
> wandering in the mystic rhythm
> of jungle drums and the concerto.[7]

Mbella Sonne Dipoko makes a beautiful statement about our growing up, our passage from the life of uncles and fathers and mothers, from our "world of greenness," to the world of today:

> And the mind soon flung pebbles at the
> cranes of the off-shore island.
> But today
> Floods flee the rising sun
> And the owls hoot from the edge of the dark song
> Like cripples blinded by sandy winds
> Dreams drift under the low sky of our sleep
> And our hearts listen to the voice of days
> in flight,
> Our thoughts, dusting the past.[8]

Dennis Brutus on the police raids that harass him and his fellow blacks in South Africa:

> Investigating searchlights rake
> Our naked unprotected contours;
> over our heads the monolithic decalogue
> of fascist prohibition glowers
> and teeters for a catastrophic fall;
>
> boots club on the peeling door.
>
> But somehow we survive
> severance, deprivation, loss.

7. Moore and Beier, *Modern Poetry from Africa,* p. 122.

8. Mphahlele, *African Writing Today,* p. 201. Reprinted by permission of Mbella Sonne Dipoko.

Patrols uncoil along the asphalt dark
hissing their menace to our lives,
. . . .
but somehow tenderness survives.[9]

Because of the very nature of prose narrative, the novel does not *directly* express a state of mind like poetry. Although we talk prose, poetry more closely approximates the human voice as an expression of feeling and state of mind; as long as we do not try to let rhetoric do this for us. And yet the sense of commitment is no less sharp among the novelists. They document even as they dramatize. The abler kind of novelist allows for a free play of irony too. The following themes are very African:

(a) the conflict between new ways of life, new beliefs and the old (Chinua Achebe, Onuora Nzekwu)
(b) the homecoming of the black man who has been schooling overseas (Lenrie Peters, William Conton, Camara Laye)
(c) agitation against ruling white settlers (James Ngugi)
(d) the politics of independence (Camara Laye, James Ngugi, Ayi Kwei Armah)
(e) humiliation set in a colonial situation (Ferdinand Oyono, Achebe)
(f) labor upheavals (Sembene Ousmane, Peter Abrahams)
(g) black childhood and schooling (Laye, Bernard Dadié)
(h) the black servant (Oyono, Mongo Beti)
(i) the student in metropolitan capitals of colonizing countries (Dipoko, Dadié, Aké Loba)
(j) city life (Cyprian Ekwensi, Wole Soyinka)
(k) snobbery among the enlightened blacks (Soyinka)
(l) oppression by whites, urban squalor, physical violence, police terror, etc. (Alex la Guma, Peter Abrahams, Bloke Modisane, Richard Rive)
(m) themes drawn from mythology (Amos Tutuola)

9. Dennis Brutus, *Sirens, Knuckles, Boots* (Ibadan: Mbari Publications, 1962). Reprinted by permission of the author.

(n) traditional life and the coming into consciousness of the village boy (Legson Kayira, Adhambi Asalache)

All these writers reflect a sense of commitment: the writer is committed to the African setting; he does not show any indication of wanting to flee from his African origins in preference for the Western world. He does not imagine a world of fantasy as an escape from his real environment. If he has to lead the life of an exile, his creative instincts still drive him to African themes that demand his commitment, or those in which he has already taken a stand. He is often nostalgic. Propaganda is subdued in our fiction, with the outstanding exception of *The African* (William Conton), which obviously advertises African values, and *Wand of the Noble Wood* (Nzekwu).

We do not yet have in African fiction anything like George Orwell's manner of thrusting his prejudices and hates into the open. I think this spoils his fiction. That *Animal Farm* and *1984* have stood the test of time can only be due to the fact that the political situations the propaganda in these works is aimed at still exist today. The prevailing political moral of the books still holds. We do not yet have a George Orwell in Africa perhaps because the writer here is still by and large ambivalent in his attitude toward Western values, and by the same token his experience is richer. Even when we advertise Africa or lash out at white oppression, our commitments tend to shift slightly when we are not simply documenting. Our stand on South Africa is at bottom only relatively firm. A self-avowed Marxist like Alex la Guma writes more like Gorki and the American Negro than Orwell. He documents and "shows" without throwing in asides to let his voice be heard (except at a few unguarded moments). And yet you know where La Guma stands. You know he wants to demonstrate the wickedness of a social system in which the black man is trapped. This is the social realism we have become accustomed to in Negro-American literature which portrays a similar human situation.

I have tried to show the various distances and degrees of commitment without attempting to be categorical about whether propaganda should or should not enter a work of art.

Yet I do not even think this is the question: rather it is the manner in which the writer uses propaganda that decides the literary worth of a work. The question of the audience also comes in. For instance, poetry inspired by *négritude* is for an elite, because only the elite are plagued by the problem of identity. Such a poetry is only meant to be read by such people and appeal to them. It does not speak to or about the unassimilated masses, except in a romantic idealistic way. But in the Caribbean and the United States I can see how relevant such poetry is even for the masses. Because, especially in the U.S., the Negro is in a state of siege culturally. He has to locate himself as a Negro with a double commitment: to share in the life of the Americans as a whole, and to assert his cultural importance, so that he is not integrated into the white culture on the white man's terms.

As we find ourselves eventually talking about commitment, Leon Trotsky's incisive and perceptive remarks in his *Literature and Revolution* come to mind:

> Our Marxist conception of the objective social dependence and social utility of art, when translated into the language of politics, does not at all mean a desire to dominate art by means of decrees and orders. It is not true that we regard only that art as new and revolutionary which speaks of the worker, and it is nonsense to say that we demand that the poets should describe inevitably a factory chimney, or the uprising against capital! Of course the new art cannot but place the struggle of the proletariat in the center of its attention. But the plough of the new art is not limited to numbered strips. On the contrary, it must plough the entire field in all directions. Personal lyrics of the very smallest scope have an absolute right to exist within the new art. Moreover, the new man cannot be formed without a new lyric poetry. But to create it, the poet himself must feel the world in a new way. . . . No one is going to prescribe themes to a poet or intends to prescribe them. Please write about anything you can think of! The form of art is, to a certain and a very large degree, independent, but the artist who creates this form, and the spectator who is enjoying it, are not empty machines, one for creating form and the other for appreciating it. They are living people,

> with a crystallized psychology representing a certain unity, even if it is not entirely harmonious. This psychology is the result of social conditions. The creation and perception of art forms is one of the functions of this psychology. . . .
>
> The proletariat has to have in art the expression of the new spiritual point of view which is just beginning to be formulated within him, and to which art must help him give form. This is not a state of order, but an historic necessity. You cannot pass this by, nor escape its force.[10]

I should like to think that African *négritude* propaganda, even in its limited framework and with its special audience, has at least prompted, in a social context, those who need it to search for a new spiritual point of view which we need to give artistic expression while at the same time we strive to explore the human situation in general. Black pride need not blind us to our own weaknesses: in fact it should help us to perceive our weaknesses. Also, I do not care for black pride that drugs us into a condition of stupor or inertia. I do not care for it if leaders use it to dupe the masses so that they forget to clamor for the bread and decent shelter and education they have a right to.

Can the major concerns of Africa merge at any point with the universal major concerns like war, poverty, fascism, the insolence of power? Must they indeed merge? It is quite obvious now that the African writer (even outside South Africa) has arrived at the "threshold of pain" where he can already begin to feel the muscle of political authority in his own country. And so the Russians and the South Africans are not alone. I hate to think that one of these days we are going to sink to the degenerate level of Afrikaans writers in South Africa who have always censored themselves and not dared to challenge the government, because it has Calvinist Boer origins, like themselves, because they are all of a tribe.

What Trotsky has to say about the Russian situation has

10. Leon Trotsky, *Literature and Revolution* (Ann Arbor: University of Michigan Press, 1960), pp. 170–171. Reprinted by permission of The University of Michigan Press.

relevance to Africa, although things in his country are not what he had hoped for. The Russian proletariat would be a parallel of our illiterates and semi-literates, urban or rural. Russian proletarian poets could be paralleled by our new intelligentsia writing today, using the language and craft of the former colonial power. Trotsky says that the proletarian poets used versification as a means of complaining of one's sad fate, or expressing revolutionary passion. During the revolution they wrote to a march, which was quite simple. After the tension of the civil war, these poets had to approach poetry as an art and as a craft. But they did not have the background the bourgeois intelligentsia had who had appropriated literature and created a tradition in it. The proletarian poets were not artistically prepared. Their poems still read like revolutionary documents. When they were faced with the problems of craftsmanship and art, they began to seek for themselves a new environment. "It does not look as if the present groups of worker poets are destined to lay immutable foundations for a new great poetry. Maybe distant generations, yes. For there will be plenty of ideologic and cultural deviations, waverings and errors for a long time to come!" This is Trotsky's assessment.

I cannot agree with Trotsky's prescription that the new art should be incompatible with pessimism and "all other forms of spiritual collapse." Also, I am not sure how, if we must, we can make our art "virtually collectivist." What we do know is that we have not yet adopted a view of the world as we see it in Kafka, which the Marxist critic George Lukacs despairingly refers to as being "from the perspective of a trapped and struggling fly." "This experience," he adds, "this vision of a world dominated by *angst* and of man at the mercy of incomprehensible terrors, makes Kafka's work the very type of modernist art. . . . Kafka's *angst* is the experience par excellence of modernism." No black hero in Negro-African fiction is stricken with *angst* which makes him dash about like a trapped fly. Perhaps he is the typical hero of Western literature, perhaps he is the supreme example of modern man as modern literature sees him because the Western world today is both a disintegrated and a differentiated one. So it produces disintegrated personalities. We have not yet created societies like this in Africa, and the heroes of our fiction cannot yet be seen as possessing what one may call the intensive "other individuality" of a Kafka or a Camus hero. The African hero is still very much part of a communal world. I can't even be sure that we shall stay out of Kafka's and Camus's world for all time. I am inclined to stake a lot on the dialogue that is continuing between the stream of modern life in Africa and the stream of its *living* traditions. Each is informing and criticizing the other, and this dialogue may yet determine the idioms of the literature to come. At the moment our literature in the European languages is of a frontier kind. We are pioneers at the frontier, seeking a definition of ourselves and the past from which we have come. The frontier lies between us and the white man's technology, religion, mores, economics, and so on. We try to address him and ourselves at the same time.

All the same I go along with the rest of Trotsky's thesis. I think we need to think seriously about what he has to say about culture also. In traditional society where culture is a process of growing up and is not a thing separate from human activity in general, comfort and abundance would not be necessary for the growth of culture. But we have poverty and illiteracy, wealth and literacy unequally distributed. So Trotsky's formula for the Russians may very well be ours as well. He wrote in 1924:

> Culture feeds on the sap of economics, and a material surplus is necessary, so that culture may grow, develop and become subtle. Bourgeoisie laid its hand on literature, and did this very quickly at the time when it was growing rich. The proletariat will be able to prepare for a new socialist culture and literature not by laboratory method on the basis of present-day poverty, want and illiteracy, but by large economic and cultural means. Art needs comfort, even abundance. Furnaces have to be hotter, wheels have to move faster, looms have to turn more quickly, schools have to work better.[11]

11. *Ibid.*, pp. 9–10.

Censorship in South Africa

In 1969 Laurence Gandar and Benjamin Pogrund, respectively editor-in-chief and reporter of the *Rand Daily Mail,* were tried and found guilty in the Johannesburg Supreme Court on two counts of contravening the Prisons Act. The charge was that they had published false information about prisons without taking reasonable steps to verify its accuracy.

The trial was a sign of the times: the forces of fascism were on the march. South Africa is a country where there is no freedom of assembly, association, or movement. White judges frequently administer the same laws differently for blacks and whites, and there are laws that apply to blacks and not to whites.

But in that trial the white man was in the dock. When this happens, and it is quite clear that the particular white man was championing the African's cause, the government bares its teeth. It feels it is dealing with a dangerous species of white man, one who must not be allowed to incite Africans, or to open the eyes of the white community and the world in general to the barbarism the black man is subjected to in South Africa. It won't do for some white moral sensibilities to be outraged; it's bad for "white unity," or the illusion of it.

The *Rand Daily Mail* reported a macabre tale of the sordid conditions African prisoners have to endure—beatings, torture

---

This essay originally appeared in the first anniversary issue of *Censorship Today: A Review of the Continuing Fight for Free Speech,* II, No. 4 (August–September, 1969), pp. 4–16.

by electrocution and other means, solitary confinement, lack of hygiene, sodomy, and so on. It is quite clear from what the accused said that they did not feel guilty about having published the reports and would do it again if they felt prison conditions still warranted it.

The South African government passed the Prisons Act knowing that African prisoners were being brutalized. The Act prohibits any press reports of prison conditions from being published unless a paper has made sure that such reports are correct. But more often than not it is impossible to ascertain this with prison authorities.

The press has been shut off from several news sources in South Africa; sources to which the public has a right. Every government has news media that coo praises to it as well as those that are critical of the Establishment. The South African government is fond of vilifying the English-language press, while the curly-haired boys of the *Dagbreek, Die Burger, Die Transvaler*—Afrikaans-language papers—are fondly indulged by every member of the government. The latter papers operate on the principle "Our government, right or wrong."

Mr. Horace Flather, editor of an English-language paper in Johannesburg, said in a speech in January 1963: "While the newspapers of this country operate in the shadow of many statutory restrictions, they nevertheless—largely because of their moral courage—*do* enjoy a wide measure of freedom. They do not flout or defy the laws; they simply take it upon themselves to interpret them . . . in terms of the spirit rather than the letter. And so far this practice has been tolerated by the authorities, even if rather sourly and grudgingly."

Surely one hardly requires moral courage if he merely reports facts, or protests within the law. This is in the true tradition of South African white liberalism, which has always accommodated itself in the safe capsule of legality; and that means white legality, since the laws are made by whites only. The *Rand Daily Mail*'s open support of the African cause, short of incitement to violence and sabotage and of upholding the principle of one man one vote, is a departure from this comfortable moral courage. Its exposés are a most significant milestone in the history of anti-apartheid publishing. Its courage won't necessarily advance the black man's struggle, but it is significant for the white man's own salvation.

Newspapers that struck at the roots of apartheid and courageously supported an African revolution quickly fell under the guillotine of the Suppression of Communism Act (which established the idea of a statutory Communist, ignoring whether or not the person has any relationship with international communism. Other acts gave the President power to impose unlimited censorship in all black reservations; prohibited the publication of anything that might engender feelings of hostility between races (in the broadest possible sense); and made it an offense to encourage people to repeal or break a law. In addition, several activities of the press became illegal under the Public Safety and Sabotage Acts. One concession exists under the Sabotage Act: it is left to the newspapers to decide what they may or may not publish. If their judgment offends the Department of Justice, they are liable for prosecution.

Press censorship spills over into yet another and far-reaching Act of Parliament—the Publications and Entertainments Act, passed in 1963. The Suppression of Communism Act of 1950 already empowered the Minister of the Interior to ban any periodical (including any newspaper that he thought was promoting the spread of communism, was published by an unlawful organization, or was serving mainly to express the views of such an organization). A Government Notice of February 1963 prohibited certain categories of persons from being office-bearers, officers, or members of any organization which in any manner prepares, compiles, prints, publishes, or disseminates any newspaper, magazine, pamphlet, book, handbill or poster, or which assists in doing so, unless special permission is given.

The Publications and Entertainments Act of 1963 set up a Publications Control Board to examine any publication or film submitted to it, and to investigate any entertainment which is declared undesirable by either the Board or *any* other person.

Among other things, a publication is deemed undesirable if it or *any part of it* is indecent, obscene, offensive, harmful to public morals, blasphemous, offensive to the religious convictions of any section of the inhabitants of the Republic, brings any section of the inhabitants into ridicule or contempt, is harmful to the relations between any sections, or is prejudicial to the safety of the state, the general welfare, or peace and good order. The phrase in italics above means that a work shall not need to be judged as a whole—a restriction that certainly runs counter to the ideas that lie at the center of art.

If in the opinion of a court of law a publication is likely to displease or corrupt the minds of people likely to see it, or treats in an improper manner of matters that subvert morality, such a publication will be deemed undesirable. It is illegal to publish or import or produce such material after it has been declared undesirable in a prosecution.

The Board must also approve of a film before it can be shown publicly. But the Board may allow the showing of a film to one specified group, race, or class and not to another. A film is subject to the same criteria for acceptability as journals, books, posters, and so on. Add to these criteria the restrictions against a film if it depicts the President, the armed forces, public characters, crime, or lust, in an offensive way, or if it shows controversial or international politics, scenes of violence involving white and African persons, or the intermingling of black and white.

Films showing American Negro achievements are not seen by African audiences. When *The Glenn Miller Story* came to South Africa, the Louis Armstrong scenes were excised bodily from the film before African cinemas could show it. Films like *The Defiant Ones, A Man Is Ten Feet Tall, Guess Who's Coming to Dinner,* and *In the Heat of the Night* could never be shown to black audiences. It is most doubtful whether they will ever be shown to white audiences.

While a person or persons aggrieved by the Board's decision about a publication may appeal to a court of law, he can only appeal to the Minister of the Interior about a film.

The Act also seeks to control public entertainments, whether they are commercial or are meant to contribute to a fund or are restricted to the membership of an association. If an entertainment offends the religious convictions or morals of a group or runs contrary to the public interest, it will be prohibited. Appeal against the Board's ruling lies with the courts.

Several organizations and individuals protested this law in all its stages. One hundred and thirty South African writers and fifty-five painters and sculptors submitted a Declaration of Principles to the Minister of the Interior against the measure. They stated: "Nowhere does this law provide that the nature and intent of a literary work should be considered as a criterion of judgment. . . . Writers who must publish inside the country are liable to be forced either into silence or superficiality—with fatal consequences especially for Afrikaans literature." Afrikaans literature, like Bantu literature, is published entirely in South Africa, while most English-language writers publish in Europe and the United States.

One outstanding Afrikaans writer, Andre Brink, warned in February 1969, on the fifth anniversary of the Publications and Entertainments Act, that South Africa's young writers and thinkers will not accept this "tyranny of the spirit" indefinitely.

Among the many books that have come under the ban are those by Brendan Behan and John O'Hara; books published in the Penguin African Library series; Colin and Margaret Legum's *South Africa: Crisis of the West;* South African writing by whites, like Nadine Gordimer's *A World of Strangers* (paperback, the hard-cover edition still being allowed) and *The Late Bourgeois World;* Wilbur Smith's *When the Lion Feeds;* and Stuart Cloete's *The Turning Wheels.* The banned also include Robert Graves's *King Jesus;* Bertrand Russell's *Why I Am Not a Christian;* Ralph Ellison's *Invisible Man;* Sinclair Lewis's *Kingsblood Royal;* Sartre's *The Age of Reason;* Bellow's *The Adventures of Augie March;* Nabokov's *Lolita;* Martin Luther King's *Stride toward Freedom;* Steinbeck's *The Wayward Bus;* James T. Farrell's trilogy, *Studs Lonigan;* Aldous Huxley's *Island;* and some of Faulkner's and Baldwin's books.

The ban was lifted in the last two years on D. H. Lawrence's *Aaron's Rod* and *Love among the Haystacks;* two books by

James Hadley Chase; Robert Graves's *I, Claudius;* Hemingway's *Across the River and into the Trees;* Kathleen Windsor's *The Lovers;* Carl Burke's *God Is for Real, Man;* and Maxine Davis's *Sex and the Adolescent.*

Since the Publications law came into force in November 1963, between ten thousand and fifteen thousand titles, mostly published outside the country, have been banned as undesirable, objectionable, or indecent. In 1967 alone, four hundred and nine imported publications and twelve local ones were banned. In 1968 four hundred and nineteen imported publications and twenty-one local ones were banned. And, under the Customs Act of 1955, reading material could be lumped with goods that could be impounded by Customs if they were deemed objectionable. The Film Censorship Board that existed before 1963 was replaced by the Publications Control Board. And under the Suppression of Communism Act of 1950 and the Riotous Assemblies Act of 1930, amended several times, plus the Prisons Act of 1959, publication of any periodical or other reading material was forbidden if it was thought to be spreading communism or engendering feelings of hostility between blacks and whites. Usually all political journals of radical dissent against apartheid, leftist or not, were killed this way. It is a crime to be found in possession of any such banned material or to disseminate it.

It is not an offense to be found in private possession of banned books under the Publications Act. But it is an offense for a bookseller to keep a banned book for sale and for a librarian to distribute or exhibit it.

The Publications Act forbids the publishing of utterances, verbal or printed, of persons who have been banned; i.e., prohibited from attending gatherings of more than eight persons, and from moving outside a magisterial area. Any speech or utterance or writing or statement made *anywhere* at *any time* by a banned person may not be printed, published or disseminated or recorded or reproduced by mechanical or other means. The late Albert Luthuli, former president of the African National Congress and Nobel Peace Prize holder, who was a banned person, could not be quoted in South Africa. Similarly, Ronald

Segal (writer of *The Americans* and other books), Ruth First (writer of *One Hundred Seventeen Days* and other books), cannot be quoted. In December 1968, five hundred and seventy-nine people, black and white, were living under banning orders and restricted to certain magisterial areas. They could not enter any factory or educational institution and could not be quoted in the country. Twenty-three Africans were living in banishment away from their homes and could not be quoted. Sixty-three South Africans living abroad could not be quoted, nor could those—numbering over seven hundred—who were in the country and had been named statutory Communists. Then there were also over a hundred persons living in exile who were either connected with a banned political movement or were unattached but writing, who could not be quoted or published in South Africa. All African writers living in exile were included in this list. Inside the country itself, the two main African political movements have been declared unlawful and therefore silenced.

Publications coming from overseas have to be scrutinized by booksellers for any statements made by banned persons. Once several hundred copies of the London *Sunday Times* had to be removed from newspaper stands when the news agency concerned discovered that they contained comment by Mr. Nelson Mandela, former leader of the African National Congress now serving a life sentence in prison on Robben Island. The copies could only be sold after the paragraph had been blacked out.

The two-pronged thrust of the Publications Act is aimed at sex morals as portrayed in literature and at politics as a literary theme. A negligible number of books in South Africa portray sex in anything like lurid terms. It is the political ethics the authorities want to control and direct. As Nadine Gordimer, the South African novelist, says, "Politics is a dirtier word than sex, so far as our censors are concerned." She also says, with warranted despondency: "For all writers of South African literature, truncated already, the future is written between the lines in the Government Gazette list week by week. The present much-vaunted thaw in the political climate may be warming the toes of spectators at rugby and cricket matches, but it has not reached the cold storage in which much of our creativity lies. We are not to doubt. We are not to question. We are not to inquire. We are not to allow our characters to speak their right thoughts—or yours or mine. Local publishing firms stick to carefully vetted biographies and safari adventure. Our literature in English, that a few years ago was hailed with some justification as remarkably lively and questing, is in danger of degenerating into accepting the role of art as an embellishment of leisure. Any piece of writing that thrusts deep into life here will find itself not in the bookshops and libraries but in the desk drawer, waiting, as the work of many writers did in Germany and Russia, for times to change and for the dialogue in which truth begins to be heard again. Only then shall we be able to speak of a South African literature." [1]

Although various other acts could prosecute a newspaper for publishing undesirable material, under the Publications Act the South African Press Union (association of newspaper proprietors) drew up its own code of conduct. Individual employers may decide whether or not to accept it. A Board of Reference exists, made up of two managerial nominees and a retired judge, who is chairman. It oversees reports to insure acceptable standards of accuracy and decency. Editors or journalists who are considered to have violated the code may be reprimanded by the Board, and this act will be published by other papers. The final clause of the Code reads: "While the press retains its traditional right of criticism, comment should take cognizance of the complex racial problems of South Africa, the general good, and the safety of the country and its peoples." [2]

Here lies one of the saddest dilemmas of the ruling white minority in South Africa. The majority of the white community want to maintain their fat feudal comfort. A few would like the black man to enjoy some of it, but not on the latter's terms, otherwise it won't look like the gesture of generosity it is

1. Nadine Gordimer, "South Africa: Towards a Desk Drawer Literature," *The Classic,* II, No. 4 (1968), pp. 73–74.

2. Muriel Horrell (comp.), *A Survey of Race Relations, 1962* (Johannesburg: South African Institute of Race Relations, 1963), p. 59.

meant to be. The African can only work outside the Constitution in order to bring down the structure of white supremacy entrenched in that Constitution: he has no voice in parliament and had no part in the making of the Constitution. The white man who throws in his lot with the blacks must, like them, either exile himself or end up in jail. The white man in the newspaper business who would like to avoid being banned can only buzz frantically, like a fly beating desperately about in a tight enclosure, just to assert his right of protest. The newspaperman's dilemma here resembles that of the university students who have been demonstrating against the South African government's whittling down of academic freedom. They have declared that they will protest *within the law*.

Not all newspaper owners accepted the terms of the Code. Associated Newspapers did so under protest, announcing that they would withdraw later if necessary. They added: "While the concept of self-discipline by the press is acceptable, the Board (of the Association's directors) believes that political pressure has given rise to the establishment of the Board of Reference. . . ." ("Political" implies government pressure.) This is clearly the spirit in which the *Rand Daily Mail* pushed out a little nearer the danger point, short of supporting sabotage and a bloody revolution.

The complaints that the Press Board of Reference has dealt with in connection with alleged violations of the Code show quite clearly that the English-language and the Afrikaans-language papers in the country are ranged against each other, representing two factions of the Establishment, with the former group at least buzzing dissent noisily if circumspectly. Meanwhile Afrikaner nationalist party congresses have kept the heat on, trying to persuade the government to take action against the English-language press.

The latest venture in this direction, although veiled in its intentions, is that announced by the Minister of the Interior, S. L. Muller. He promised new legislation to remove the exemption given to the Newspaper Press Union by the Publications Act. "Certain newspapers and journals," he has said, "appear to have no regard for codes of conduct." He said he hoped the announcement would contribute to "greater responsibility and greater cooperation on the part of the press." It was the duty of the government, he insisted, to protect the moral values of the people. The Minister would have us believe that what worries him is "sensational reporting and sex," which are supposed to dominate certain publications. The government had to intervene, he said, where the "freedom of the press degenerates into indifference, recklessness and abuse." And yet none of the fifteen complaints lodged since 1962 with the Press Reference Board of the Union had anything to do with sex. They dealt with politics and erroneous reporting.

Once the exemption goes, it means that the Press Union will not operate its own code of conduct; the press will then be subject to the direct censorship of the Publications Act. A professor of sociology at the Afrikaans University of Pretoria has recommended serious thought before such a law is passed. Obviously, although the Afrikaans-language press does not want to oppose the Minister openly on such legislation, its fear of outright censorship prompts it to insist that the Minister should be anxious about sex and sensation. Says an English-language paper, "We all know what politicians mean by 'sensational' reporting. How often have news reports been described by politicians as 'distorted,' 'inaccurate,' 'sensational' or 'out of context' one week, only to be proved a week later accurate in detail."

By and large Afrikaans academicians try to make a virtue out of necessity by establishing theories that will justify press censorship. Professor G. J. Pienaar of Potchefstroom University (Western Transvaal) has had a doctorate thesis passed in which he blames the press for the restrictions the government is imposing on communication media. Professor Pienaar is chairman of journalism at his university—the only department of its kind in the country. He complains that the press is sensational and relies on clichés like being "the watchdog of democracy and freedom" and "representing the public." He observes that censorship pressures have intensified with the increase of tension inside South Africa brought about by the cold war and growing African nationalism, by the souring of the country's relations with the rest of the world. Professor Pienaar comments further: "This sharp attitude has to do with the refusal of a large section of the South African press, and especially those who through their language are more easily understood by the outside world, to write in such a way that material which could be regarded as harmful and subversive to the country does not appear in print."

Dr. Pienaar traces statutory censorship back to the three ancient civilizations—the Hebraic-Christian, Athenian, and Roman, on which the South African community is founded. By this he means, of course, the *white* community. Press exposés of irregularities, he asserts, are of great value for any society so long as they do not intensify suspicion between government and people.

Every so often journalists are excluded from any scene the reporting of which the authorities may regard as explosive or too revealing. Political commentator and poet Anthony Delius was permanently excluded from the press gallery of the House of Assembly because he had allegedly shown contempt of Parliament—he had commented on the removal of portraits of the British Royal family from the walls of the House. Permission is refused for an indefinite length of time to journalists to enter African reservations (holding not less than 3 million souls) during crises ranging from anything like famine to political rioting. The late Robert Kennedy's entire entourage of reporters could not accompany him during his visit in the country. There are international reporters who are forbidden permanently to enter South Africa.

The South African Broadcasting Corporation (SABC) is a public corporation and a monopoly run by public funds in license fees. Its current affairs program has again been attacked by the English-language papers for its political bias. In 1965 it refused the South African Institute of Race Relations permission to broadcast a commentary on its Council meetings. But the Afrikaans counterpart of the Institute, the South African Bureau of Racial Affairs, was permitted to broadcast a program on its 1965 Congress. The Christian Council of South Africa was denied an opportunity to disprove charges made about the policy of the World Council of Churches, which the Dutch Reformed Church (the church of the state) has always accused of a misplaced liberalism and even communistic bias. Certain personalities have also been refused a chance to reply to attacks made on them on the current affairs program. So have organizations like the National Union of South African Students, which is predominantly English-speaking and has often incurred the government's antagonism by opposing apartheid in institutions of higher learning. It was at its invitation that the late Senator Robert Kennedy visited South Africa.

The South African Society of Journalists passed a resolution to the effect that the SABC should be a forum of public opinion rather than the major mouthpiece for government propaganda. This arose from the sustained vitriolic criticism of the Society mounted on the current affairs program. The Society, which is opposed to the government's policies, was not allowed to reply on SABC. Subsequently, the SABC admitted on current affairs that one of its purposes was to counter views presented in the English-language press.

The Broadcasting Corporation runs programs from Radio Bantu aimed at African listeners. A company has installed in several municipal houses cheap radio sets that can only receive broadcasts from Radio Bantu, i.e., only what the government wants Africans to hear. Most of the 2 million inhabitants of the Transkei reservation can only afford FM radio sets. Again, they listen only to what the authorities want them to hear—in the people's own language. The Transkei has been flaunted by the South African government as an "independent Bantu homeland," whereas in fact the educational system, radio, defense, immigration, overseas travel, passports, the treasury, and the laws fall under the jurisdiction of the central authority of the Republic.

Intellectual freedom in South Africa exists only in the sense in which an overseer of an outdoor prison can tell a man he is free to run away and then, when the prisoner makes a dash for it, he is gunned down—for attempting to escape. Afrikaans universities instill a sense of both supremacy and superiority into their students. You cannot teach this without at the same time making an equally conscious effort to teach Africans to accept a position of inferiority. In 1952 I was dismissed from teaching by the South African government, together with two colleagues of mine. We had been campaigning against the recommendations of a commission that the education of the African should not give him the idea that he can be an equal of the white man. The schooling he had been receiving (British-oriented and steered mostly by mission institutions) alienated him from his own people and frustrated him because, as the structure of society stood, he could never compete with the white man. Having arrived at this premise, the commission concluded that the African should be taught in the medium of his tribal vernacular. His curriculum was curtailed so that, where before he used to write the same examinations as the white student, he had now to be assessed by separate and lower-level standards.

In history, social studies, and civics the black pupil had to be taught to accept as facts the hypotheses that the white man came to South Africa to civilize savage indigenes; that the black man was underdeveloped, and that the white man was to remain his lifelong Christian trustee; that passes were necessary to control the movements, labor needs, and urban influx of Africans; that white superintendents and commissioners were necessary as heads of rural and urban administrations in African areas; that the black man was immature and could not exercise the vote nor represent his people in Parliament. Thus inquiry was to become taboo in African education.

After us several hundred other African teachers were summarily banned from teaching when the Bantu Education Act came into force, incorporating all the principles in the commission's recommendations. We could not appeal to any court of law. A black teacher, even in his private capacity, is no longer allowed to write or utter any kind of criticism whatever of any public servant of any rank.

The lowering of elementary school standards was to affect secondary schooling and university standards. Entry of non-whites into white universities is now forbidden. Tribal colleges have been established in ethnic areas where both blacks and whites teach, but only after thorough screening by the government. The Minister of Bantu Education directly oversees these colleges, whereas white universities have autonomous administrative councils. The Minister has to approve the membership in the students' unions. Political statements from either staff or students that criticize the authorities are forbidden. An Afrikaner Nationalist spokesman declared before the tribal colleges were set up: "The proposed colleges should have a religious basis and . . . a religious character. It is my heartfelt conviction that we cannot, for example, allow these institutions to be anti-religious or anti-Christ. . . ."

Of the existing tribal colleges, the Minister of Bantu Education stated: "Where one has to deal with underdeveloped peoples, where the state has planned a process of development for those peoples, and where a university can play a decisive role in the process and direction of that development, it must surely be clear to everyone that the state alone is competent to exercise the powers of guardianship."

The tribal colleges write examinations of the University of South Africa, which has been catering to both white and black by correspondence courses. It means that the black student is at a disadvantage, because he has to write the same examinations as the white student but without the same degree of preparation at lower levels as his white counterpart.

I felt stifled in my own writing after I had been dismissed from teaching. It seemed that the last leverage had been wrenched from my grip, although even as a teacher my activities had been circumscribed. In trying to express our views about the kind of education we felt our people were entitled to, we were in a sense trying to survive our ghetto existence. In trying to make a run for it, so to speak, we were gunned down.

After five years, I decided to leave my country. Other black writers also left: playwright Alfred Hutchinson; novelists Can Themba, Alex la Guma, Bloke Modisane, Lewis Nkosi, A. C. Jordan; poets Raymond Kunene, Dennis Brutus, Arthur Nortje; and satirist Todd Matshikiza. Themba, Jordan, and Matshikiza have since died. Subsequently we were all, with the exception of Nortje, declared "prohibited immigrants" in South Africa and listed as writers whose utterances and writings cannot be quoted or read in the country. During those days in South Africa, when we saw the dark clouds massing in the sky as a warning of the storm that was to break upon us in the form of the Bantu Education Act, I thought much about my childhood. I thought of those early days in a bush school when one began to recognize the written word in a reader. The words leapt like fire in front of one, seemed to splutter and send off sparks to illuminate so much of the world depicted in the reader. In the upper classes one became aware of much more, and even life in a squalid urban ghetto generated its own energy, which destroyed some and hurled others onto the steel gates of white privilege. And when the white man heard the gates shake, he knew he was never going to enjoy a quiet sleep. And because you were not going to stop pushing, he was going to have to bring out his gun. He was going to have to reinforce his barricade with laws to prevent you from agitating, protesting, by word of mouth or by the written word. He did all this—and more.

I used to think then, "What has it all been for—that discovery that began the quest?" Only since I came out of the nightmare have I stopped quarreling with the illogic that led to the discovery. I have begun to realize all the more fully what the dread of censorship can do to the intellect.

Nadine Gordimer wrote in a Johannesburg weekly in 1964: "During the past ten years, South Africa has lost many English-speaking writers and intellectuals generally, including the entire nucleus of the newly emergent black African writers. . . . If I, or any other English-speaking white South African, should leave my homeland, it would be for the same reason that those others (i.e., the whites) have already done; not because they fear the black man, but because they grow sick at heart with the lies, the cheatings, the intellectual sophistry . . . sick of the brutalities perpetrated by whites in their name."

The white writer can still get away with a lot in South Africa. A black man who wrote the same things the liberal-minded among the whites write, who represented the same liberal and egalitarian ideas, would most likely be banned. As long as a white man speaks up for this underdeveloped person, it is not bad; it is in the true tradition of South African white liberalism. True enough Alan Paton cannot travel abroad, nor can playwright Athol Fugard. But Paton's books are not banned, nor Fugard's plays. Nadine Gordimer is not restricted, although two of her novels are banned. Nor is Paton banned within the boundaries of the Republic.

And yet their position has its agonies, because they have decided to stay. Fugard says, "I think I can go on producing plays under segregation (mixed audiences are not allowed), even admitting some non-whites to private readings. But eventually I may have to take a stand like Paton's (i.e., a certain degree of political commitment). We are in a corner. And all we can do is dodge here and push there. And under it all there's a backwash of guilt." And how can there not be guilt when a playwright is prepared even to sneak in non-whites through the back door?—an act that is elevating to neither of the two people?

The Afrikaans writer and the African writer who uses a Bantu language are in the same situation. Afrikaans and Bantu poetry blossomed about the same time—during the second half of the nineteenth century. Both languages are published only in South Africa, except for the Bible, which is published in Bantu and Afrikaans outside South Africa as well. No writers have been banned. Bantu writers of the last two decades have been writing with the school readership in view. Most Africans, even after school, have been reading English both because of the glorious feeling of triumph at being able to read it and because so much of the external world they have mastered or are mastering comes to them in English. Also, the insistence of the government on the use of the vernaculars as media of instruction in school encourages writers to address themselves to this readership. Their books have to be censored by white school inspectors, so that no political material that is adversely critical of white society can pass. It seems that we have seen the last of the Bantu novel of the first four decades of this century, which had an adult appeal.

The Afrikaans novel, even the kind that comes from a group called the Sestigers (those who emerged in the 1960's), including Etienne Leroux, Jan Rabie, and Andre Brink, hardly touches the fringe of the dilemma in black-white relations. The writers are part of the community that pushed Afrikaner nationalism to the present frontiers. They criticize the government more by word of mouth or in the press than through their creative writing. Their literature treats of human problems far removed from the actual racial conflicts that permeate all South African life. They tell us that they are rebellious against "dead tradition and worn-out symbols," that censorship is the deadweight of Puritanism. But all they do is create new symbols; they do not challenge the principles of apartheid, or they get trapped in mere eternal verities. While the Bantu writer is afraid of the written law of censorship, because he is naturally afraid of arrest, detention, and banning, the Afrikaner writer is afraid of both the written law and the sanctions of the tribe, which operate deep down in the subconscious.